Elitism

By the same author

Elites in Australia
(by John Higley, Desley Deacon and Don Smart)

Elitism

G. Lowell Field
and John Higley

Routledge & Kegan Paul
London, Boston and Henley

First published in 1980
by Routledge & Kegan Paul Ltd
39 Store Street,
London WC1E 7DD.

Broadway House,
Newtown Road,
Henley-on-Thames,
Oxon RG9 1EN and

9 Park Street,
Boston, Mass. 02108, USA.

Set in 10/12 Linotron Times by
Input Typesetting Ltd,
London
and printed in Great Britain by
Redwood Burn Ltd,
Trowbridge & Esher.

British Library Cataloguing in Publication Data
Field, George Lowell
  Elitism.
  1. Elite (Social sciences)
  I. Title II. Higley, John
  301.44'92   HM141   79–41648

  ISBN 0 7100 0487 7

Aug '81

Contents

Preface

Preferences, and beliefs resting on them, usually pervade inexpert thought, just as they pervaded all thought in the pre-modern period. People commonly interpret factual matters according to their preferences and then spend most of their time arguing that these preferred interpretations are, or should be, true. Very largely, what one wishes were true determines what one judges to be useful knowledge. In social thought at least, the possibility that matters contrary to our preferences might be true is seldom explored seriously.

Nearly four centuries ago, the physical and life sciences and the technologies to which they have contributed emerged from this unproductive and self-deceptive mode of thought. Their practitioners did so by finding grounds for belief other than their wishes and by largely excluding preferences and normative considerations from formal discussion. However, this 'value-free' position was itself possible only because, at the time, all could readily assume that an increase of factual and causal knowledge in the physical and life sciences would be universally beneficent. Thus there needed to be no serious discussion about whether means of prolonging life, reducing pain, increasing food production, or providing substitutes for human labour were to be welcomed. Until very recently, in other words, physical and life scientists did not face the difficulty of recognizing that some possible knowledge not seen to be useful from the standpoint of the preferences and beliefs that underlay the scientific enterprise might still be true.

No such simple way of abandoning false knowledge and acquiring reliable knowledge was available to the social sciences. Social scientists could clearly and unambiguously discuss the subjects of their studies only if they all overtly or covertly assumed some more or less universal moral standard. But apparently there is no common human point of view about social behaviour that is similar to the one that served the physical and life sciences during

their initial advance. This is so because of the conflicts of interest
between persons and groups that inevitably arise from material
scarcities and from probably inherent social scarcities of such
things as respect, status and belongingness.

In the social sciences, and now in some areas of the natural
sciences, there are different moral points of view. These strongly
determine the expected usefulness of particular knowledge and,
consequently, whether it will be seriously investigated and, if true,
found to be so. Thus social scientists identifying with a body of
slaves would not consider the discovery of psychological techniques for keeping slaves submissive an advance in knowledge,
and they would not work to discover such techniques. Given that
social and political knowledge can be used to the disadvantage of
some persons, social scientists who happen to hold those persons'
points of view, or to sympathize with them, will consider that it
is better that such knowledge not be known. In brief, compared
with the physical and life sciences, the backwardness of the social
sciences may be accounted for by their practitioners' intermingling
of diverse moral points of view with factual matters, as well as by
their failure to adopt such points of view as might open the way
to the reception of such knowledge.

One such point of view that ought to be adopted seriously is
that of the successful, participative and allegiant person in a modern national society. This is the person who is confident of his
ability to conduct his relations with society in personally satisfying
ways. From his point of view, but not from other points of view,
elitist questions may seriously be asked, for example, 'To what
extent and in what respects is political and social power necessarily
concentrated in a few persons in all societies?' As this question
indicates, in current social science 'elitism' refers to factual concentrations of power and influence. In this usage, 'elites' need not
be better or cleverer than 'non-elites'.

Persons whose circumstances make them self-confident and self-
reliant may seriously ask this or similar questions because they
are prepared to accept any likely answer as useful knowledge. By
contrast, such questions cannot be asked seriously from the point
of view of the unsuccessful, the excluded, and the disallegiant
person. The latter individual feels that, unless it is greatly
changed, the society to which he belongs offers him no real satisfaction. He cannot seriously ask an elitist question because he

cannot accept as useful knowledge any answer other than a very specific one that offers some clear road to social transformation.

Since there is almost certainly some necessary amount of power concentration in all societies, whether it is relatively much or relatively little, the elitist question stated above, and the larger intellectual position it reflects, presumably offer a way of advancing social knowledge. One who can honestly ask the question can also accept the answers that investigation might bring. Thus a frank pursuit of social knowledge from an elitist point of view would very likely be more successful in accumulating knowledge about social and political structure than the social sciences have so far been.

Yet in the history of the social sciences those practitioners who have been most successful, content, and allegiant have seldom asked any serious elitist questions. Those who did pursue knowledge in this area generally did so while adhering, at least vaguely, to a range of egalitarian points of view. Most commonly, the active social scientist has been an 'intellectual', not just in the sense of a learned person but also in the sense of a social critic. He has been strongly, if sometimes ambiguously, attracted to the democratic, socialist, and anarchist currents of modern social thought. These became seriously influential in the late eighteenth century after it appeared that scientific knowledge would greatly improve the average conditions of human life and after some fortunate societies were able to practise representative government with fairly extended suffrage. Thus the typical social scientist has hardly been fully allegiant to the society in which he has lived and worked. Though often comparatively well off, he has usually not seen himself as among the fully successful in his society. Consequently, though he might raise questions relevant to the elitist position, his point of view has tended to exclude from the category of useful knowledge a large number of possible answers.

We are not saying that past or present social scientists were or are so alienated from their societies as to be inevitably driven to consider only egalitarian rather than elitist hypotheses. We merely point out that, given the existing current of opinion during the past two hundred years, social scientists have tended to identify with, and have sought to sponsor and encourage, general egalitarian positions. This was especially easy to do under the guise of the 'value-free' position which they imported from the older sciences. Adopting this position made it unnecessary to analyse seriously the value positions tacitly carried over from general social and political alignments and sympathies. Yet these unanalysed commitments tended to define the range of conclusions that social scientists were prepared to consider as constituting useful knowledge.

Thus the history of social science has been a decidedly preferential search for explicative principles that are immediately and directly supportive of aspirations to a more equal society and polity. But either because the facts are hostile to these aspirations or because there is no simple sense in which the facts support them, the progress of social science has been limited. It is on the basis of these considerations that we recommend in this book a more serious consideration of elitist hypotheses as a way of advancing social knowledge in a professional social science sense. At the same time, we are equally concerned to show that a much more explicitly elitist viewpoint or orientation among persons in influential positions generally is necessary to meet the current problems of developed and developing societies realistically and practically.

Given our contention that the willingness to pursue elitist questions and hypotheses depends to a substantial degree on one's social circumstances, we would be remiss if we did not give a brief resumé of our own situations. We write as academics who are fortunate to have enjoyed reasonably secure and decently compensated positions in universities that have imposed few tasks upon us that we would not have voluntarily undertaken. Our work has been in large part self-directed. We have interacted regularly with colleagues on the basis of mutual respect, deference and substantial equality. We have lived all our lives in countries that have been able to protect us against material deprivation, cultural discrimination and political subjugation. Our privileged circumstances have enabled us to prefer and to work for humane and reformist policies and styles of political leadership. Obviously, our interests lie in perpetuating these or similar circumstances for ourselves and our associates. We have always hoped to see roughly comparable circumstances enjoyed by as many persons throughout the world as social and political possibilities allow.

We wish to thank our numerous colleagues in the University of Connecticut, in the Australian National University and in several other universities for their comments and suggestions about drafts of this book's chapters and related material. In particular, Ms Desley Deacon, in the Department of Sociology of the Research School of Social Sciences at the Australian National University, deserves special thanks for critically reading, discussing and helping to edit the entire manuscript. Mrs Betty Gamble and Ms Vivien Read gave us excellent typing assistance throughout. Finally, we are grateful to Professor F. Lancaster Jones and the Department of Sociology at the ANU for inviting Field to spend the first part of 1979 in Canberra so that we could complete the book without inconvenience.

G. L. F., J. H.
Canberra
March 1979

Chapter 1

Elitism in eclipse

There was one period in the history of modern social science in which a substantial and promising elitist position was articulated. This was during the first third of the present century, and the principal figures involved were Gaetano Mosca, Vilfredo Pareto, and Robert Michels.[1] All three wrote extensive bodies of elitist political theory. All three were much more interested in the scientific explanation of how politics occurred and of the limits to political change than they were in promoting any political position for its own sake. None was consistently hostile to the general Western liberal value system, though more orthodox thinkers in Western countries have made much of the fact that all three tolerated, in the sense that they did not politically oppose, the Italian Fascist regime. Of the three, Pareto is perhaps least accepting of Western liberal values, but he is not an advocate of any other cause. Michels is an ex-democrat and ex-socialist, initially disillusioned, as he believes, on factual and not normative grounds. As his career progresses, Mosca concedes more and more the desirability and propriety, but not the effectiveness and viability, of liberal and, as he would punctuate it, 'democratic' government. Presumably, the Central European background of these men made it easier for them than for their Anglo-American

1 For Mosca's central work, see Gaetano Mosca, *Elementi di Scienza Politica*, Bari, Gius. Laterza, 1953 (2 vols, 5th ed., Preface by B. Croce), and in English, G. Mosca, *The Ruling Class*, New York, McGraw Hill, 1939 (ed. A. Livingston, trans. H. D. Kahn). For Pareto's political sociology, see Vilfredo Pareto, *Scritti Sociologici*, Turin, Unione tipographico editrice torinese, 1966, or in English, V. Pareto, *Sociological Writings*, New York, Praeger, 1966 (ed. S. E. Finer, trans. D. Mirfin), or V. Pareto, *The Rise and Fall of the Elites: an Application of Theoretical Sociology*, Totowa, N.J., Bedminster Press, 1968 (ed. H. L. Zetterberg). For Michels's leading work, see Robert Michels, *Political Parties: a Sociological Study of the Oligarchical Tendencies of Modern Democracy*, New York, Collier Books, 1962 (trans. Eden and Cedar Paul, Introduction by S. M. Lipset).

and Northern European colleagues to admit the probably mistaken character of popular Western political creeds.

Mosca stressed the somewhat ambiguous point that those who rule are always a small minority in any society regardless of its formal organization. He commented at length, in a generally cultivated and liberal fashion, on a wide variety of historical polities, but he did not develop a formal system of analysis. He emphasized the desirability of what he called 'juridical defence', a concept roughly analogous to that of civil liberties. In a strict sense it meant judicial institutions independent enough to prevent persons in power from penalizing their rivals merely to further their own political chances. Though he denied its ideological rationale, and though he doubted its ability to persist, Mosca showed much sympathy for representative government, particularly in his later writings.[2]

Pareto, an engineer who turned later in life to economics, where he made substantial technical contributions, eventually also turned to political sociology, where he attempted a systematic theory of social and political change. In particular, he stressed changing combinations of the characteristics of ruling elites, the behaviour of which he likened to that of lions and foxes. In addition, he sketched the circumstances under which one elite combination, if it were not gradually absorptive of outsiders, would collapse and be replaced by the other.

Michels contributed a cogent analysis of what he took to be the inherent conflict between leaders and followers in a complex society. His example, with which he was personally familiar, was conflict in the German Social Democratic Party before World War I. He showed that even in such an avowedly egalitarian organization an elite of party leaders and officials necessarily became in most respects middle-class in attitude. By their presence in strategic positions, without which the organization would lose effectiveness, they came to dominate the organization and to modify its policy in directions more congenial to their interests than to those of the mass membership. His general conclusion was that oligarchy is inevitable in all organizations – the so-called 'iron law of oligarchy'.

2 See, for example, his so-called 'Final version of the theory of the Ruling Class', written in 1933 and reprinted in James H. Meisel, *The Myth of the Ruling Class: Gaetano Mosca and the Elite*, University of Michigan Press, 1962, pp. 382–91.

Pareto, Mosca, and Michels regarded themselves as empirical social scientists rather than social philosophers. They could do this because the acceptance of elitism as a moral point of view and as a respectable intellectual orientation was not uncommon in their milieu. Especially in Central Europe at that time there were many overt elitists. Throughout Western civilization, moreover, there were certainly many persons in the educated public who sympathized with this point of view. The three writers therefore felt no strong need to argue the moral respectability of their position in order to get a hearing. Although they often adopted polemical styles, these were intended to denigrate what they regarded as wayward intellectuals, in particular Marxists, and not to publicize an entirely novel point of view. In this general situation, they thus were able to direct their efforts to clarifying the mechanisms of elite behaviour and to making the elitist position more operational.

A half-century later this is no longer the situation in which advocates of elitist models find themselves. At present there are very few avowed or conscious elitists or, for that matter, persons who are open-minded about the employment of elitist models. Supporters of a laissez-faire economy, in so far as they can still be found, merely posit that this is the best route to increased prosperity for all. Social science advocates of the so-called 'democratic theory of elitism' are mainly concerned to make the comfortable argument that while elites play a role in the governance of modern societies this role is neither unpleasant nor irremediably opposed to a substantial degree of democracy. Those who discover power elites and ruling classes in these societies nearly always temper their ostensibly factual observations with their personal beliefs that there should not be, and possibly need not be, such perversions of democracy and equality. In fact, all associate themselves more or less fully with egalitarian and democratic values, and for many publicists 'elitist' is a favourite pejorative.

Thus to advance elitist hypotheses today it is not enough merely to argue, as Pareto, Mosca and Michels could, that elites always or usually exist and that they are probably of decisive importance. In addition to this, it is now necessary to refute the widely held assumption that values such as equality, liberty and freedom are universal and objective. Probably only by making this refutation can contemporary thought be brought to see the importance and the propriety of elitist assumptions. For if values are not universal and objective, but are instead plural and conflicting, then it will be seen to follow that only some tolerance of arbitrary, vested rights and powers, however impossible they may be to justify on an *ab initio* basis, constitutes a plausible and very likely a necessary barrier to the profitless battle of all against all.

I

During the half-century from roughly 1925 to 1975, the elitist paradigm sketched by Mosca, Pareto and Michels received very little elaboration. In Germino's view, only Guido Dorso, a relatively obscure political scientist who died in 1947, tried seriously to extend it.[3] This effective eclipse of the elitist paradigm can be largely accounted for by the novel historical experience of Western societies during the later nineteenth and first half of the twentieth centuries. These years probably offered the most disorienting and deceptive circumstances that history has ever laid before a major civilization. Their consequence has been a set of basic considerations about human needs and behaviour that came to be generally believed by educated persons after World War II and that still underlie most thinking about social problems and policy choices in Western societies. Yet these basic considerations are all more or less erroneous.

Prior to the eighteenth century in the West, and down to the present day in the rest of the world, human experience has almost always taught that societal survival in a world of scarce resources cannot be assumed. The claims of rival societies for territory and for resources have had to be considered an ever present threat to domestic well-being. In the face of such threats, societal survival is more nearly in the interest of every person than is the pursuit of any general rearrangement of statuses and rewards within society. This is because it is usually obvious to most persons that defeat by rival peoples, to which internal social conflict could be expected to contribute, would probably result in the loss of their own culture and, consequently, in culturally degraded statuses, if not in outright enslavement and extermination.

But from at least 1683, when the Turks were defeated before

---

3 See Dante Germino, *Beyond Ideology: the Revival of Political Theory*, New York, Harper & Row, 1967 (chap. 6). Dorso's work is also discussed by Meisel, op. cit., pp. 365 ff.

Vienna, the preponderance of military skills and armaments pos-
sessed by Western societies has kept them largely free of this
special nightmare. All subsequent attacks on their home territories
have been unleashed by other Westerners, not by foreigners from
drastically different cultures. These attacks have hardly ever been
seen as threatening cultural or societal extinction. Gradually, this
circumstance made it possible for Western populations to become
preoccupied with programmes for internal social transformation
of a more or less revolutionary character. Indeed, this became a
central interest in Western thought. While opinion differed about
the difficulties or disasters that such transformation might cause
because of its threat to entrenched domestic interests, it was
possible to avoid seriously considering the importance of social
peace for the very survival of Western societies in a world of rival
peoples. In other words, the assurance of cultural and societal
survival for Western civilization in general fostered the probably
deceptive belief that drastic social transformation, mainly in an
egalitarian direction, could be purchased at an acceptable cost.

During the past century or so, the spurious plausibility of this
aberrant current of Western social revolutionary thought was reinforced by a second deception. This was the doubt that the progress
of scientific knowledge and its technological applications cast upon
the universality of material scarcity. Prior to the latter part of the
nineteenth century in the West, it was always fairly obvious, just
as it still is obvious in developing societies today, that desirable
positions in life are so few that the persons holding them can be
expected to resist utterly all attempts at their displacement.
Indeed, it was fairly obvious that this resistance would be so
vehement as to make efforts at sweeping social change dubiously
profitable, quite apart from the openings they might give to invad-
ing foreigners.

No matter of what they may consist, desirable positions almost
always mean superior status, and this is usually accompanied by
a hold on more than an average share of a society's material
wealth. In developing, less productive societies it is easy to see
that a relatively equal distribution of material wealth would leave
all persons seriously deprived. From the middle of the nineteenth
century, however, Western industrialization and increased productivity seemed to offer possibilities for a much more equal
distribution of material goods exactly because the consequence of
universal deprivation appeared to be less and less certain.

For about a hundred years, Western progress did remove ever larger proportions of Western populations from the immediate threat of misery. In varying degrees and at different times, productivity increases actually appeared to be reducing emulative motives among various strata. For example, during the 1950s and early 1960s in North America and Western Europe it was not difficult to believe that progress in material well-being had basically satiated mass desires for better material circumstances. During those years in particular, increases in material affluence were rapid enough to outrun conscious consumer demand and, concomitantly, to suspend the forceful assertion of self-interest on the part of population categories that were previously, and for the most part remained, relatively poor.

These circumstances created the widespread impression that redistribution out of surplus production would shortly bring about a practical equality. This impression ignored, of course, the non-material aspects of stratification, just as it ignored the engineering and economic difficulties of sustaining unlimited growth. Eventually, however, after a few Western populations reached very high levels of material well-being without coming appreciably closer to a practical equality, the illusory character of this impression became clearer.

This historical overview helps us to understand why, shortly after World War II, a moral point of view and an intellectual orientation that were compatible with the elitist paradigm ceased to be effectively transmitted to the young in the leading Western countries. In fact, they began to disappear with the deaths of the persons who held them. Of course, even before the war in countries such as the United States, Great Britain and France there had been no general acceptance of the elitist paradigm. A whole variety of circumstances, in addition to the two main ones we have just reviewed, combined to make it seem unduly pessimistic in those countries even during the first half of this century. Perhaps it is enough to say that because these were the most powerful and the most obviously successful countries in the West, persons who lived in them were necessarily more optimistic in evaluating their domestic political and social prospects.

During the pre-war years, nevertheless, many thoughtful persons could readily acknowledge at least some features of the elitist paradigm as true. This was especially so when they turned their attention to earlier historical periods or to the less developed regions of the world. Specifically, during the pre-war period it was fairly widely surmised, and often openly stated in well-informed circles, that what the Americans, the British or the French called 'democracy' in their own governments – the relatively free competition for elective offices that carried real authority – was a luxury. To be sure, 'democracy' was something to be firmly cherished by the countries that could afford it, but it was a luxury none the less. Thus it was widely noted that opponents of government policy were allowed to speak freely and that the results of elections were generally respected precisely in those countries in which no very sweeping policy changes were seriously at issue. It was widely assumed, moreover, that sweeping changes could only be imposed by force on large and unwilling categories of any nation's population.

From roughly the end of World War II, however, even this willingness to take seriously and to discuss at least some aspects of the elitist paradigm effectively ceased in the leading Western societies. As the post-war period proceeded, fewer and fewer people could be found who were prepared to revert to, or even grudgingly concede the partial validity of, elitist hypotheses. Thus the change that set in after World War II was real and significant. The major aspect of this change was a new paradigm that came to pervade Western thought and that made the elitist paradigm very difficult to contemplate at all. This may best be called the 'welfare state paradigm'. It appeared spontaneously immediately after World War II in the thinking of some elites in the leading Western countries and Japan, and over a decade or so it became generally professed. It amounts to an amalgam of the remnants of liberal and socialist doctrines once each of these had been stripped of its realistic and more pessimistic considerations.

II

During the first half of this century, the thought of Western-educated persons prevailingly followed two elaborate but distinct paradigms. In general, those who were most individually powerful were thoroughly imbued with liberal conceptions, while those who were more disaffected or dissatisfied adhered to socialist views. Both paradigms were, by this century, rich in detail and nuance. The eighteenth and early nineteenth century models from which they derived had been the subjects of lengthy elaboration and exegesis. Along the way, both had absorbed much of the practical political wisdom of earlier intellectual traditions. Both assumed a certain tendency in human behaviour toward individualistic selfishness. The liberal paradigm proposed ways of harnessing this tendency in order to make it a principal means of progress, in practical terms through the freedom of private entrepreneurs from political controls over the production and distribution of goods. On the other hand, socialism saw the same tendency toward selfishness as something that adequate social organization could and should suppress, also in the interest of progress, a goal which, in the abstract, overlapped considerably with that which liberals called by the same name.

Until World War II the liberal and socialist world views were sufficiently contradictory that co-operation between adherents of both always presented grave moral problems. In the early years of the Weimar Republic, socialists, because they also thought of themselves as democrats, joined in some coalition majorities for fear that otherwise there might not be majorities to support the democratic political system. But they found this experience extremely distasteful because it made them appear to be assuming responsibility for a capitalist system that they were powerless to change. Similarly, on two occasions the British Labour Party had the unsatisfying experience of forming governments that lacked absolute majorities in parliament. They thus found themselves compelled to govern a capitalist system that they had no mandate to change. The second of these two occasions led to a deep party split and to the party's repudiation of most of its best-known leaders. During the decade before the war, socialist cabinets in Sweden and Norway enjoyed somewhat more favourable situations, but they too lacked sufficient parliamentary support to enable them to pursue anything like a full implementation of their programmes.

For their part, liberals gravely doubted their own ability to accept such a mistaken notion as socialism even if it were to win a majority at the polls. While an important part of socialist thought insisted on following democratic procedures where they were well established until socialism should be victorious in a popular vote, socialists too doubted that their liberal opponents would accept their authority even after they had won an election. Some socialists, concentrated mainly in the so-called communist parties, were unwilling to respect the authority of 'bourgeois' governments even if these governments could claim formal endorsement by popular majorities.

Thus during the inter-war years and earlier any discussion of serious social change, which was always viewed in terms of a change from a capitalist to a socialist economy, inevitably raised questions about the possibility or the propriety of some upset in the formal machinery of democratic government in the countries where representative politics were well-established. The important point is that always and inevitably in such political speculation the possibility of independent elite action, whether in favour of the right or the left, had to be considered. In this way, up until World War II, the relevance of the elite paradigm, and awareness of it, were preserved.

But already in the inter-war years the ground for a coming together of liberalism and socialism after World War II was being laid. Part of this ground was the rise of communist and fascist movements. A socialist faction, to which the specific label 'communist' was soon applied, managed to seize and hold power in Russia as that country staggered under the costs of its participation in World War I. Within a few years this regime came to be accepted as a permanent feature of the political landscape. Eventually, it satisfied the traditional criterion for socialism by abolishing the private entrepreneurial function. But, in the process, its denial of traditional political liberties and its highly dictatorial policies deeply offended many socialists as well as liberals. Fascism, both in its original Italian form and in the more sweeping German version, was a populistic reaction to egalitarian threats. It did not have a serious intellectual tradition behind it, however, and it could not be identified as either liberal or socialist. Consequently, its rise as a new and wholly unexpected force deeply frightened both socialists and liberals. In fact, as World War II approached, the Russian communists' efforts to organize anti-fascist coalitions brought communists, other socialists, and liberals together in short-lived governments in France and Spain.

Nevertheless, in general the inter-war atmosphere allowed little ground for a compromise between liberalism and socialism. This was especially so in the continental countries where the two ideological positions were held in their most fully developed forms. To the traditional socialist, freedom for the entrepreneur meant unemployment and exploitation for the working man. To the traditional liberal, abolishing entrepreneurs meant the non-functioning of the market, the allocation of all products by the state, and an almost inevitable political dictatorship in order to maintain sufficient authority.

But even then a limited basis of compromise had been offered in the theories of John Maynard Keynes. These purported to allow government regulation of a 'free' economy through purely fiscal policies. In the United States the full socialist ideology was known and accepted only in limited circles and there was instead a populistic tradition that had long argued for a limited and regulated capitalism. This circumstance helped the Roosevelt administration eventually to endorse Keynesianism and to begin a policy that basically presumed a capitalist economy, albeit one that was modified by Keynesian measures to control the business cycle and to allow various methods of income redistribution. Before the viability of such a policy in peacetime could be fully tested, however, it was absorbed into the war economy of World War II.

Between 1940 and 1945 the horror inspired by the German Nazi regime brought socialists and liberals together in many countries in an effort to win the war or to wage a resistance struggle under German occupation. In Britain the Labour Party eventually joined in war-time coalition with the Conservatives. The threat of fascist conquest was a sufficient motive for ceasing to question for the moment the fiscal arrangements by which entrepreneurs were rewarded. On the other hand, the overriding need to prosecute the war effectively prevented liberal opposition to measures that tended to equalize material sacrifices. Even in the United States, which was remote from the actual fighting, there seems to have been some modification of the distribution of income in an egalitarian direction. In the desperation of the fight against a universal enemy, a largely administered and directed economy was seen as necessary. Under these circumstances socialists and, once the German Nazis attacked Russia, even the communists could co-operate with liberals with little difficulty.

III

The war ended in 1945 with a regime in power in the United States that was widely believed to have squared the economic-ideological circle. That is, it had instituted an economic system that was not purely capitalist, as witnessed by the fact that it was bitterly and widely reviled by the more traditional laissez-faire liberals. But, in essence, private enterprise still prevailed and there was no serious practice of the supposed hallmark of socialism, namely government ownership of business enterprise. A somewhat similar economic system had also been instituted by a socialist government in Sweden, which had managed to stay out of, and to profit from, the war. In their more desperate conditions, the European belligerent countries had widely resorted to various expedient combinations of private enterprise and state-administered operations. Thus it was much more difficult after the war than before it to see socialism and capitalism as incapable of some, possibly desirable, intermixture. In addition, the prestige that accrued to the United States for its immense material and technological contributions to Allied victory gave some credence among educated Europeans to the comparatively imprecise American ideological tradition.

Yet, in the war's immediate aftermath, many Europeans feared that the war-time destruction of their productive plant and the presumably impending cessation of American material support would make most of the ex-belligerent countries ungovernable. It was widely believed that the demoralized European peoples would readily associate themselves with the Russian communist regime. This possible danger was averted by the Americans' pledge to rebuild Europe's productive plant, to the extent this was necessary, at their own expense. This was done with extreme rapidity and with astonishingly favourable results in a period of three or four years.

The rebuilt European economies were, of course, largely capitalist, in part because of the American influence in the rebuilding process. They began a rapid industrial production of low-priced consumer goods for mass consumption along the lines of the previously unique American pattern of mass production during the inter-war years. Given that the United States continued to pioneer in this direction, the result in the early 1950s was a rapid increase in standards of living on both sides of the Atlantic. In short order, the recovering Japanese economy, also under heavy American influence, began a similar performance.

The principal effect was to create a sudden demand for the labour of many relatively poor persons, at least as regards healthy male family heads. For the moment wages, in terms of the goods that could be purchased with them, seemed to be on the increase in all the developed countries. Consequently, for a short time much of the attention of socialism's usual supporters was diverted to private matters having to do with the acquisition of material goods. Improved housing, better clothes, and various forms of transportation and recreation – first bicycles, then cars, and in the more prosperous countries even motor boats – became available to economic categories that could not previously have considered such indulgences.

In spite of continuing misery in such quarters as the aged and female-headed families, therefore, there was comparatively little interest in social transformation during the 1950s. Socialists in Europe and the equivalent 'New Deal' Democrats in the United States began to consider seriously that their followings might be in the process of passing to the conservative camp. In the United States General Eisenhower was twice elected to the presidency, and in all European countries south of Scandinavia electorates supported right-of-centre governments during most of the decade.

Two important changes of policy accompanied the post-war productivity increases. First, a much more general acceptance of collective bargaining between trade unions and the employers became the norm in all Western societies. Second, systems of social insurance to provide against the contingencies of life, such as old age, unemployment and medical expenses, were widely instituted or extended in coverage either on a general basis through the public treasury or more selectively under various collective bargaining agreements. While these policy trends were initially opposed by many conservatives, this opposition was sharply and quickly truncated by the generally favourable business conditions that entrepreneurs and managerial personnel continued to enjoy.

Thus by the late 1950s it was possible to consider that the pre-war economic and social systems of Western countries had been modified markedly. Further, it was apparent that this had been done with the support of relatively conservative political forces. There had come into existence a system operated mainly by capitalist firms but one that was considerably modified by the redistributionist measures associated with social insurance and with collective bargaining. It appeared to be generally acceptable to all major factions, and analysts became absorbed in the description and explanation of the 'welfare state' and of a condition that was apparently its by-product, the so-called 'end of ideology'.

In any full sense of the term, ideology had certainly not ended. But there had occurred a large deflection of elite attention away from the prescriptions of the two well-established ideological paradigms, liberalism and socialism. However, these previously diverse labels continued to be accepted.[4] Most educated persons still thought of themselves as located in one or the other of these two broadly differing political categories. The major change was that from roughly 1955 to 1965 adherence to one or the other symbolic camp made little difference for the policies espoused. To the extent that they approached or held positions of real power, socialists lost interest in their formerly distinctive aim of altering the ownership of productive firms. They were content to allow, and even to administer, a generally capitalist organization of production as long as certain mildly redistributionist measures were practised. Liberals largely abandoned strict laissez-faire principles. They were willing to accept a large degree of state control over the economy and to concede considerable power to trade unions as long as entrepreneurial and managerial incomes remained high. In effect, a new and common ideology, welfare statism, had, as regards both intellectual principle and policy prescriptions, largely supplanted previously held socialist and liberal positions.

IV

As an ideological position, welfare statism has been extraordinarily meagre in its contents. At the most, it merely counselled major factions to accept a political settlement of their long-standing antagonisms. But the settlement it urged was wholly unplanned, never seriously analysed, and it was in fact feasible only in the accidental and momentary circumstances of the post-war period. It involved socialists and liberals forgetting what was previously meant by their ideologies and accepting instead a fortuitous combination of capitalist enterprise, strong trade unionism and fairly comprehensive social insurance programmes. By contrast, previous liberal ideology had long recommended and rationalized

4 The exact terms differed. In the United States 'liberals' were called 'conservatives' and the nearest thing to 'socialists' were called 'liberals'.

much more detailed decision-making, and this was true of previous socialist ideology also.

In its essence, this welfare state 'settlement' entailed the assumption by taxpayers and other, mainly business, interests of certain social insurance obligations, as well as the making by capitalist firms of various concessions to trade union demands in collective bargaining. This was politically acceptable because, at the time, the immediately foreseeable costs of these obligations and concessions appeared to be easily absorbable out of increases in productivity. However, as the recession of the middle 1970s eventually demonstrated, the settlement was always a precarious one because its political acceptability in a country having many prosperous people could readily be upset by demographic and other social changes that materially increased the burdens which it imposed.

During the 1970s, this was in fact what began to transpire. Faced with technical limits on increased material productivity, with social and psychological limits on their ability to multiply attractive and authoritative work positions, known in the vernacular as 'meaningful' jobs, with a demographic trend increasing the size of the normally dependent age cohorts in their populations, and with a bid by Third World countries, notably successful in the case of petroleum, to seize for themselves some of the previous income sources of the Western countries, all the developed societies (with perhaps the temporary exception of Norway) were trying to meet increased redistributionist claims with reduced resources. This could only result in drastic inflation or serious cutbacks in the levels of public services to which their populations had become accustomed.

The welfare state ideology has literally nothing relevant to say in this contingency. In fact, its intellectual status as the ideology that comprises the only general considerations present in the minds of political and administrative leaders is dangerous and harmful. Unlike the previous ideologies of socialism and liberalism, it fails entirely to warn leaders that people do not voluntarily accept disadvantages for the benefit of strangers unless they are convinced that they have no better alternative. On the contrary, welfare statism presumes that most persons and groups, especially when they are already quite prosperous, are inclined toward some considerable altruism in bargaining with others. Thus it invites open confrontation between potentially hostile interests on the assumption that outcomes moderately favourable to all are possible.

Worse, welfare statism does not counsel the leaders of opposing interests to assess their means of action beforehand and to formulate their retreat positions. Instead, it contains the naive belief that successful bargaining depends mainly on healthy communication. It denies the historically valid observation that bargaining outcomes ultimately reflect little more than the respective powers of the negotiating parties to coerce each other. In a further confusion of reality, it assumes that the settlements reached through bargaining would also be reached if the same or related matters were put to a democratic vote. This gives to welfare statism a veneer of democratic respectability, but it also blurs the line between popular and elite actions. This is a confusion, of course, because bargaining presumes conflicts of interests, while democratic voting and other forms of popular participation presume some substantial degree of common interest.

Thus the main harm of welfare statism is the invitation that it offers for naive issue confrontation at the popular level without prior elite analysis. This is exemplified domestically in developed societies by the increased incidence of wildcat and other strikes in circumstances that are likely to injure middle-class persons either as bystanders or participants. For example, sudden stoppages of air and other transport, which are now common, result in the drastic disruption of personal plans and interests. Protracted and bitter strikes of school teachers, postal carriers, power station operators, sanitation workers and the like, none of them any longer rare, have serious disruptive consequences. Even more ominous is the outbreak of fierce labour disputes involving the police, notably in New York City and Montreal in recent years. These may involve disorders perpetrated by demonstrating officers or open invitations to robbers to operate with impunity at certain times. Even when finally settled, these disputes leave a residue of bitterness and distrust between police and citizens that prevents necessary refinements of police services.

Such strikes demonstrate the fundamental difficulty of collective bargaining once it is extended beyond the competitive manufacturing plants that are more or less insulated from the rest of society by the operations of the market. This is that in service and public sector occupations coercion in bargaining must eventually escalate to treat the whole community as a hostage or, even, as the enemy. Ultimately, the logic of such developments is to open the way to the domination of politics by those with the last word in coercion, namely the military forces.

It is the ascendancy of the welfare state ideology that makes active harassment of the public by air controllers and pilots, by police and fire-fighting forces, by postal and hospital workers, by schoolteachers and civil servants seem inevitable. Under any even slightly more realistic ideology, major efforts to obviate such outcomes would have been made years ago. Possibly the leaders of these groups would have themselves exercised more restraint. Almost certainly elites that were more realistically oriented would have seen, long before open defiance occurred, the extreme danger that the mere proliferation of undifferentiated, but vital, mass services constituted at a time of sharpening competition for increases in income levels. At least, they hardly would have placed so much reliance on the altruism and 'good sense' of these groups as guarantees of self-restraint. They would certainly have moved to keep ahead of demand in the distribution of benefits to such groups. They might have found ways of separating into different career patterns such potential mass claimants on public funds as are involved in the functions of law enforcement, instructing the young, transportation and other public services.

In the international and inter-ethnic areas these same elites have allowed trends to develop to the point where hijacking airplanes, taking hostages, and inflicting random violence on rival groups and innocent bystanders have become common. Thus the conflict of Israelis and Palestinians, of Catholics and Protestants in Northern Ireland, of Moluccans and Dutch in Holland, and the various guerrilla manifestations of the North–South world conflict have been allowed to develop to points where drastic and random harm is soberly, systematically, and deliberately inflicted. Under more substantial ideologies, these conflicts probably would not have been allowed to reach present levels of confrontation without prudent concessions aimed at holding down the impulse to random violence. No doubt, given the aversion to formal warfare in view of modern weapons systems, some of this escalation has been unavoidable. But it was hardly likely to have reached present proportions if the conflicts had been appraised by elites under more realistic ideologies when they were first emerging.

It is the lack of an ideology that would lead elites to perform more adequately the function of political foresight and planning that is a principal problem for developed societies today. This is not to deny that on many matters electorates that are accustomed to authority can make sensible decisions. When the chips are down, such electorates may make as good a choice as circumstances allow. But what they cannot do is shape these circumstances by planning ahead and by warding off the escalation of issues to the point where they are too divisive to permit democratic solutions. Only elites who can apply the necessary time and steady attention to public matters can effectively do these things. However, this presumes the presence of a more self-conscious orientation toward these functions among elites than currently exists. As well, it presumes an ideology that is a good deal less threadbare intellectually as regards human motivation and behaviour than welfare statism. Thus if profitless and barbarizing forms of conflict are to be avoided in developed societies a solution to these paradigmatic and ideological dilemmas must be found.

Chapter 2
The elitist paradigm restated

'Paradigm' is a general term that most commonly refers to a specific intellectual way of looking at a matter for scientific, moral, aesthetic or other purposes. The Oxford Dictionary defines it as 'a pattern, exemplar, example'. The principal difference between a paradigm and a theory is that the set of related concepts comprising a paradigm is less rigorously specified and therefore less immediately productive of testable hypotheses. In these respects, the body of concepts about elites found in the work of Mosca, Pareto and Michels is best thought of as a paradigm. In the previous chapter, we reviewed this paradigm's contents and the reasons why it went into eclipse during the middle fifty years of this century, and we alluded to its conceptual attractiveness as compared with the seriously deficient 'welfare statist' paradigm that currently dominates thinking about social and political matters in Western societies.

Merely resurrecting the paradigm stated by Mosca, Pareto and Michels will not do, however. This is because, paradoxically, those writers placed too much emphasis on the determinant importance of elites. In their eagerness to contradict and discredit the Marxist paradigm, they contended not only that elite rule is inherent and inescapable in all societies, but that elites are essentially unlimited and unchecked, except by their own corruptions and weaknesses, in their actions and effects. Thus the paradigm they stated was 'elitist' in the most comprehensive sense. Whereas the Marxist paradigm held that all important changes in society are determined by the relations between antagonistic classes, the elitist paradigm held that elite ideas and actions are everywhere determinative of important social change.

In effect, elitism and Marxism were at loggerheads over the importance of society versus politics as *the* determinant of change. In their classic versions, Marxism gave politics little or no autonomy, while elitism said there was nothing but politics. The categorical nature of these contentions prevented both paradigms from generating effective and substantiated theories. No Marxist theory has been borne out by a series of recurrent, observable phenomena such as levelling revolutions or the disappearance of capitalist societies. Despite a hundred years' efforts to make good on its theoretical promise, Marxism remains merely one of several competing paradigms in social and political thought.

Because of its long eclipse, the theoretical promise of elitism has been less explored. Pareto's extensive treatment remains the most rigorous attempt to translate it into effective theory. While there may be some basis for claiming that the rise of European fascist regimes bore out one of his predictions, on the whole the stability and resiliency of most Western political regimes over the past half-century have confounded his concept of the seesawing struggle between different kinds of elites, the lions and the foxes. Equally important, the political decisiveness of well-documented shifts in non-elite electoral and social preferences have undermined the claim that elite politics always and everywhere determine social and political change. Like Marxism, the elitist paradigm has not produced an effective, substantiated theory.

It is therefore necessary to restate the elitist paradigm by markedly reducing the determinacy that Mosca, Pareto and Michels assigned to elites. Such a restatement would then occupy the middle ground between the classic elitist and the Marxist paradigms. The restatement that we offer in this chapter indicates where and how elites are checked by non-elites. It depicts elites as always requiring the support of non-elite groupings. Second, it portrays elites as basically limited by the appeals that they must make for non-elite support. It presumes, in other words, that the political arguments of elites must generally conform to the orientations and attitudes of the non-elites to whom they are addressed. Third, our paradigm holds that non-elites' general orientations toward the social and political world are determined by the 'level' of socioeconomic development that a society has attained. That is, different levels of development create different configurations of non-elite orientations, and these limit the themes and arguments that elites may use in their appeals for support. When elites fail to operate within these non-elite limits they risk losing their power and tenure. Finally, our paradigm holds that non-elite orientations are only manifested in very general opinion tendencies. Hence the detailed treatment of political questions is largely left to elite choice.

This interplay of elite choice and non-elite inclinations effectively prevents certain political outcomes in all societies. First, it prevents purely elite ideals from being translated into policies because such ideals cannot be readily justified to non-elite followers. Second, it prevents the attainment of purely popular ideals because elites, who do not fully share them, will not pursue the necessary policy initiatives. This means that politics in any society tends to limp along without the kind of clear aims that idealists imagine, and with minor rather than major adjustments of policy being all that is normally possible. Even in the rare case when some elite faction inaugurates an intentionally radical programme, the opposition of other elite persons and the intractability of non-elite orientations defeat any sweeping change in the structure of society.

What do we mean by elites? It is enough to say initially that elites are the persons who occupy strategic positions in public and private bureaucratic organizations (e.g. governments, parties, militaries, productive enterprises, trade union and other occupational organizations, as well as media, religious and educational organizations, various organized protest groups, and so on). Where the interest is in *national* elites, as here, these organizations are those that are large or otherwise powerful enough to enable the persons who command them to influence the outcomes of national policies individually, regularly and seriously.[1]

This conceptualization of elites means that our paradigm does not cover simple, non-bureaucratized societies, although we shall later characterize the nature of power and politics in such societies. Unlike much popular usage of the term, moreover, 'elite' is not used here to designate persons allegedly distinguished by 'superior' personal traits or skills. Rather, our paradigm focuses on the political actions of persons, normally of middle age or older, who happen to find themselves, for shorter or longer periods, in especially powerful organizational positions in complex societies.

1 We return to this conceptualization below. It is also discussed in J. Higley, G. L. Field and K. Grøholt, *Elite Structure and Ideology*, Columbia University Press, 1976 (pp. 13–19).

I

Because they are fairly fixed and definite, we begin by conceptualizing the limits that non-elite attitudes and orientations place
on elite action. The basic framework of this conceptualization is
developmental. It refers to non-elite variations during the history
of Western societies and of Japan as they modernized and rose to
what has been unexampled world dominance. Allowing for some
foreseeable differences, there is reason to expect that these non-
elite variations will largely be repeated in any Third World countries that manage to develop in the future.

There have been four distinct configurations of non-elite attitudes and orientations historically. In effect, these define four
'levels of development' conceived of in terms of the organization
of non-elite work forces. In Level 1, work forces were almost
wholly devoted to agricultural and other kinds of 'autonomous'
work such as hunting, supplying fuels, artisan and craft work. The
distinctive feature of this work was its small organizational scope.
Usually, it required no more than the co-operative efforts of
family groups, reinforced by some amount of village collaboration.
When it came to determining the timing and form of necessary
tasks, such work allowed a large amount of individual and small
group autonomy. The minimal co-operation that it required was
readily motivated by the ever present threat of general famine.

The individual and small group autonomy afforded by agricultural work and small-scale family enterprises did not normally
result in political freedom for most persons, however. Self-governing communities in Level 1 societies were always rare. Usually,
an armed and leisured aristocracy was settled on the land, forcing
the working population to support it. For the most part, the
members of aristocracies did not participate in, or closely regulate,
the ongoing agricultural, artisan and other work. They were
usually content merely to levy their incomes from the work of
others.

In our paradigm, then, Level 1 societies are characterized by
the 'undeveloped' or severely 'under-developed' socioeconomic
conditions in which most Western populations lived prior to the
sixteenth century, and in which most of the world population lived
prior to the twentieth century. It is important to note that the
absence of large-scale bureaucratic organizations in Level 1
societies meant that they did *not* contain elites in our sense of the

term. This is because without such organizations there could be no strategic organizational positions that conferred elite status. Instead, as we have noted, power in Level 1 societies was usually concentrated in a leisured, hereditary aristocracy or other ruling class.

Level 2 societies, on the other hand, have been characterized historically by incipient urbanization and the creation of a small but distinct working class assembled in industrial workshops and factories. This organization of sizeable numbers of workers under one roof necessarily meant that they had to be subjected to continuous managerial supervision, usually on the basis of wage-earning employment. This was because factory work does not permit much individual or small group autonomy when it comes to deciding the timing and forms of work tasks. Instead, factory work is planned and supervised by persons who are usually socially remote from production workers. In this respect, it frees workers from the discipline of the self-imposed tasks that are characteristic of agricultural and other autonomous work. This is why industrial workers have always been more likely than members of self-supporting peasant and artisan families to abstain collectively from work, to riot and to rebel.

The absence of a meaningful acceptance of work duties among industrial workers creates policing problems. Bureaucratic organization is required to preserve order and to supply the motivation essential to getting tasks performed. In Level 2 societies, this organization has been manifested mainly in permanent bodies of soldiers and police, in ministries engaged in tax collecting and in supplying military needs, in judicial and penal organizations, and in the usually private managements of large-scale commerce and small-scale industry. In other words, the growth of an organized manual component of the work force has necessarily involved the corresponding growth of a non-manual, bureaucratic component that has been engaged in managing and governing on a full-time basis. The emergence of both these work force components was the principal feature of Level 2 societies historically. The persons who were strategically located in the bureaucracies of such societies, and who devoted most of their time and energies to managing them (e.g. kings and ministers, military and police officers, shipping magnates and industrial entrepreneurs), became the main power-holders, the elites.

Nevertheless, manual and non-manual employed workers have

comprised only small proportions of Level 2 work forces. Most persons in Level 2 societies have continued to work in agriculture, artisanship and small-scale trading on a family basis. By contrast, Level 3 societies have been marked by a much more productive agriculture that, together with other family-scale enterprises, has engaged only about half the work force. Historically, a great many persons in the rather large industrial sectors of Level 3 societies would have been peasants in Level 2. The small working class in Level 2 thus expanded to a large category in the historic cases of Level 3. It became large enough to be culturally self-reproducing in distinct family lines, rather than consisting, as in Level 2, mainly of displaced peasants. In Level 3 societies there was a correspondingly large non-manual component of public and private sector managers, bureaucrats and service workers. In short, Level 3 societies have been characterized by the work force composition and social structure that has recently been called 'industrial'.

Level 4 societies display the so-called 'post-industrial' or 'developed' work force composition. Whereas Level 3 societies have been characterized by increased agricultural production with decreased numbers of agricultural workers, Level 4 societies have involved sharp increases in both agricultural and industrial production along with significant decreases in the number of agricultural and industrial workers. In Level 4 an immensely productive agriculture occupies a strictly minimal portion of the work force, eventually declining to less than 10 per cent. In all cases to date, the industrial manual work force has initially been fairly large, between 30 and 40 per cent. But it has declined in size even though its productivity has continued to increase. This reduction in the size of the manual component at Level 4 has stemmed from automation in the control of already sophisticated production machinery. In many areas, the only limit on the production of material objects has become the lack of consumer demand for them. Meanwhile, the large non-manual component, initially comprising about 40 per cent of the Level 4 work force, has increased still further, absorbing some of the workers no longer needed in agriculture and industry.

In Level 4 societies, however, the focus of much non-manual work is different from what it is at lower levels. In Levels 2 and 3 non-manual workers have usually been engaged in serious governing and other managerially authoritative tasks, or they have provided personal services directly to governors and managers.

But in Level 4 societies non-manual work has increasingly come to involve the rendering of services, such as education, personal care and amusement, to the general population. These tertiary activities have no material products that can be readily identified and enumerated. Thus their effectiveness can only be assessed in terms of the expectations and inclinations of the persons served by them.

This prevents one from speaking about increases in service 'productivity' in the same definite way as one can speak of productivity increases in agriculture·and industry. Indeed, it is problematic whether increases in service productivity do, in fact, occur. Some recent aggregate data cast doubt on the existence of regular increases, at least. But even if they do occur, their principal effect is to produce unemployable persons if more and more services cannot be invented fast enough to absorb the personnel who are no longer needed in the older activities of agriculture and industry. There are many signs that the invention of more and more needed, or at least acceptable, services is increasingly difficult in Level 4 societies.

To summarize, socioeconomic development has involved a shift of working personnel first from 'primary' production to 'secondary' production, and then from both primary and secondary production to service or tertiary activities. This conceptualization of the developmental process is fairly widely accepted, and it is well demonstrated by evidence.[2] However, in order to focus on variations in the politically relevant orientations and attitudes of non-elites during this process, our paradigm reconceptualizes it in terms of changes in the size of three basic work force components as demarcated by four development levels (see Table 2·1).

It is important to note that this historical pattern of development will probably not be followed in all its details by contemporary societies that are successful in developing. In particular, through the borrowing of labour-saving advanced technology, the amount of manual industrial labour required historically during passage through Levels 2 and 3 will be reduced. Instead of joining the industrial working class, therefore, persons displaced from agricultural and artisan work will be forced to take up quite indistinct

2 See C. Clark, *The Conditions of Economic Progress*, London, Macmillan, 1940; G. L. Field, *Comparative Political Development*, Cornell University Press, 1967; D. Bell, *The Coming of Post-Industrial Society*, New York, Basic Books, 1973.

Table 2·1*

Work force component	Level 1	Level 2	Level 3	Level 4
Agriculture, artisan-ship, etc.	close to 100%	about 80%	70–50%	35–5%
Employed manual industrial workers	none	4–6%	10% or more	35–25%
Employed non-manual workers	very few	10–15%	less than 30%	40% or more

* The figures presented here are illustrative. Among other things, no specification of the transitional ranges between levels is made. For the formulae by which such estimates may be calculated, and for an application of the concepts to a large number of developing societies in the past, see Field, *Comparative Political Development*, pp. 37–78.

and insecure forms of service employment in urban areas, a pattern already familiar in much of Latin America. In this respect, it may be possible for some countries to 'skip' either or both Levels 2 and 3, progressing from the 'undeveloped' configuration to the 'developed' one (albeit with a smaller manual component) in a short period of years. Kuwait seems, in fact, to have done this.

II

Different non-elite orientations toward the social and political world vary in their prevalence as societies pass through the four development levels. The extent to which these orientations are fully articulated and activated depends on the readiness of elites to make direct appeals to them and to organize social movements around them. But whether elites do or do not act in this way, non-elite orientations always tend to block those elite actions that cannot be justified publicly in terms of them. In other words, by limiting elites' abilities to justify certain policies, non-elite orientations determine what elites *cannot* do, and therefore what will *not* happen, in each development level. Within these non-elite limits, however, choosing among the several courses of action that remain open is primarily an elite function.

Central to conceptualizing non-elite orientations in this way is a modification of the Marxian view that the relations of production have a more pronounced impact on how persons perceive their worlds politically and socially than any other single factor. Where production mainly involves decisions directed toward the material environment, as is the case with small-scale agricultural and artisan undertakings, it affords co-operative, fairly equal relations among workers. Work decisions about the material environment can usually be made on an autonomous basis, and persons need not pay, or be made to pay, close attention to the decisions of others. , Consequently, workers oriented toward the material environment tend to regard close supervision by others as unnecessary interference. They tend not to comprehend or accept justifications for hierarchies in the organization of work. Except when they react defensively to external threats, therefore, workers oriented toward the material environment tend to hold an egalitarian, anti-hierarchical orientation.

All other forms of production involve work that is oriented toward the social environment. That is, they make workers dependent on social information, specifically information about the decisions made, or likely to be made, by other persons with whose work their own must to some degree be co-ordinated. This is true of both manual labour in workshop and factory conditions and of non-manual bureaucratic and service work. Especially in conditions of mass production, manual workers have no meaningful way of deciding autonomously how to integrate their work with that of hundreds or thousands of others. Additionally, they have great difficulty in perceiving production aims and of identifying with the dominant social values supporting those aims. Industrial manual work is in these fundamental respects authoritarian and alienating. More strongly than is the case with agricultural and artisan workers, it generates a rebellious, radical egalitarian orientation toward the social and political world.

Non-manual bureaucratic and service work involves an even greater dependence on social information about the actual or impending decisions of other persons. But at the same time, it allows relatively independent decision-making within sharply delimited spheres. This decision-making gives the non-manual worker some sympathy with the really powerful decision-makers in any bureaucratic organization. Moreover, both in large bureaucracies and in small service enterprises, non-manual work almost always involves the authoritative manipulation of other people. For these reasons, it generates the perception that hierarchies of authority are both inevitable and necessary features of any complex, impersonal undertaking. Non-manual work is therefore associated fundamentally with a managerial orientation toward the social and political world that is accepting of hierarchy and differentiated statuses, though not necessarily of all features of the *status quo*.

It follows from this exposition that the dominant orientation of non-elites in Level 1 and Level 2 societies is egalitarian. This orientation permeates the large body of peasants and artisans who are able to carry on their work without serious outside direction. It also permeates the much smaller group, mainly consisting of displaced peasants, who, in Level 2, work manually in supervised and directed workshops and factories. Needless to say, there is an anti-egalitarian orientation among the small body of influential aristocrats in Level 1 and among the strategically placed governing and managerial personnel in Level 2. In the eyes of most agricultural, artisan and factory workers, however, these dominant and privileged aristocrats, governors, managers and supervisors do not appear to have any obviously useful or necessary function that is relevant to everyday concerns. Nevertheless, the former may be moderately disposed to support the latter in warfare and in cultural and ethnic conflicts.

Historically, there has been a more complicated configuration of non-elite orientations in Level 3 societies. In these, the body of industrial manual workers has been large enough to transmit and perpetuate a distinctive 'working-class' culture within families. Its members have been fairly thoroughly disposed toward egalitarian standards, and in typical Western cases they have supported strong socialist political movements. Because of the substantial reduction in their numbers, and because of their increased productivity, however, agricultural and other workers in family-scale enterprises, if not actually propertied, have usually become property-minded in a serious way in Level 3 societies. Depopulation of the countryside and technological improvements have made more than a subsistence income from agricultural and from some artisan work a real possibility.

Historically, therefore, the egalitarian orientation of agricultural and other workers in family-scale enterprises increasingly came to be reserved for internal application only in Level 3 societies. Still wishing to keep their own activities as unregulated as possible, those workers tended to become highly suspicious of the more radically egalitarian, levelling aims of industrial workers and their organizations. They saw these industrial working-class aims as threatening private property and even the modest affluence that they derived, or hoped to derive, from it. Finally in Level 3 societies, the body of non-manual bureaucratic and service personnel, which is much larger in Level 3 than in Level 2, has tended to oppose any programme of sharply egalitarian social change.

These conflicting non-elite orientations in Level 3 societies have comprised an important but poorly understood paradox. On the one hand, it was only in Level 3 that conspicuous and powerful working-class political movements and organizations, which were committed to fairly extensive egalitarian change, came into existence. The paradox was that at this same point in the development sequence a less conspicuous, less organized, but no less real social majority that opposed such egalitarian aims also came into existence. This majority was comprised of many workers in agriculture and small-scale family enterprises, as well as most of the non-manual bureaucratic and service component. Although their basic orientations remained somewhat opposed, both these work force components felt threatened by the radical egalitarianism of the industrial working class. Where elites could not prevent this threat from crystallizing, it resulted in a crushing of the working class. This constellation of non-elite orientations in Level 3 societies has been the most important reason why Marxian predictions about socialist revolutions in industrialized societies have been confounded by events in all cases.

By 1600 all European societies that were seriously consolidated into what we today call 'nation-states' seem to have reached Level 2. During the late eighteenth and the nineteenth centuries, other feudal entities that became consolidated politically, and states formed through European settlement abroad that attained at least *de facto* independence (such as the United States, Canada, and those of Latin America), also reached this level. So long as these countries remained in Level 2, their politics were mainly guided by elites with relatively little non-elite involvement. In a few notable exceptions, however, elite conflict and incompetence opened the way briefly to levelling revolutions that reflected the pervasive egalitarian orientations of most non-elites. The extreme points in these levelling revolutions, what Brinton termed 'the reign of terror and virtue', were reached during the winter of 1648–9 in England, between 1792 and 1794 in France, and between

1917 and 1921 in Russia in sudden collapses of reliably centralized bureaucratic power.[3] When these egalitarian revolutions occurred, the great bulk of non-elites in all three societies were engaged in agricultural and artisan work in family-scale enterprises, although in each a small precursor of the industrial working class had appeared in urbanizing areas.

Great Britain moved into Level 3 during the late eighteenth century. By the middle of the nineteenth century the United States, the Netherlands and Belgium reached this level, and the same would have been true of northern France and western Germany if those areas had been separate nation-states. Germany as a whole, along with Italy, reached Level 3 two or three decades later when they achieved national consolidation. During the twenty to thirty years centred on 1900, most of the other countries of Western culture in Europe, Latin America and elsewhere, such as Australia and New Zealand, and one country of non-Western origins, Japan, also reached this level.

The numerical and strategic predominance of anti-egalitarian agricultural, small-scale family enterprise and non-manual workers in Level 3 made levelling revolutions, in the form Brinton described, impossible in all these societies. Yet the large size of the industrial working class and the fundamental opposition between its orientation and that of these other non-elite segments gave all these countries a high potential for industrial and political conflict as they passed through Level 3. Because they were the first countries ever to have reached this development level, moreover, the predominance of anti-egalitarian forces in them was a new phenomenon that was not fully recognized. The conflicts that resulted therefore tended to be sharper and more desperate than might otherwise have been the case. Where the intensity of conflicts within their own ranks was great, elites proved incapable of managing these non-elite oppositions. The result in Italy, Germany, Austria, Spain, Japan and elsewhere was a substantial displacement of elite persons and a thorough repression of the egalitarian minority by fascist regimes or by harsh but less ideologically populistic dictatorships that were supported, at least initially, by the anti-egalitarian majority of non-elites.

3 See C. Brinton, *The Anatomy of Revolution*, New York, Random House, 1938. It is worth noting that we do not accept Brinton's attempt to include the American Revolution, or, more accurately, War of Independence, in his revolutionary category.

There is reason to doubt, however, that countries arriving at Level 3 today will experience similarly dramatic confrontations between non-elite forces. This is because the borrowing of labour-saving technology will almost certainly make the size of the industrial manual work force component much smaller than it was in the historical cases. Moreover, the widespread unemployment and underemployment to which this technology contributes in Level 3 societies today probably has the effect of making those manual workers who are employed in modern industry a relatively privileged, well-off group. This implies that the reaction against working-class aims among anti-egalitarian agricultural, small-scale family enterprise and non-manual forces will be less sharp. In fact, the principal effect of this difference between the historical and contemporary situations of Level 3 societies may prove to be the earlier onset of Level 4 conditions in some of those now developing.

Great Britain and the United States reached Level 4 during the inter-war period in this century. But they did not fully confront the difficulties of this condition, especially the problem of maintaining high employment levels, until the 1960s. The military, bureaucratic and consumer needs of World War II, followed by the Cold War, effectively suspended the onset of these difficulties for a generation. Other countries, also affected by the Cold War, reached Level 4 during the 1950s: the Netherlands, Canada, Sweden, Australia, New Zealand, Norway and Denmark. About 1970, France, Belgium, Switzerland and West Germany also entered Level 4. Thus there has been relatively little historical experience with this high level of development, and much of the experience that there has been was modified significantly by heavy, essentially ameliorative commitments to national defence.

In Level 4 societies, as in Level 1 societies, there is in effect a single non-elite orientation in the working population. This is the orientation previously associated with the non-manual, bureaucratic work force component. In Level 4 this component is so large that normal social mobility ensures that one or more members of virtually all family groupings belong to it. Consequently, the anti-egalitarian, generally managerial orientation of non-manual workers blanks out the formerly distinctive orientations of agricultural, small-scale family enterprise and industrial workers. A generalized bureaucratic culture permeates Level 4.

The resulting lack of clear-cut divisions within the working population sharply reduces the basis for reliably differentiated social-class-based political parties and alignments. It becomes less and less clear, for instance, that a conservative majority faces a large egalitarian minority within the work force, as was the case at Level 3. Instead, conflicts develop over unemployment, centring particularly on youth, women, persons of foreign culture, and persons from other disadvantaged minority groups. Those fortunate enough to have reasonably good jobs, persons who in Level 4 societies may be called 'insiders', increasingly band together, regardless of their different occupational statuses, to fight defensively on two fronts. They seek to restrict elite actions which could eventuate in dismissals from their jobs, and they seek to prevent those currently without secure employment, the 'outsiders', from replacing them.

Two new conflicts thus open up in Level 4 societies: 'insiders versus elites', and 'insiders versus outsiders'. These replace the social class and work force conflicts common among non-elites in societies at the lower developmental levels. There are signs that these new conflicts, which until now have been peculiar to Level 4 societies, are more restrictive of elite action, and therefore more difficult to manage, than were the conflicts familiar in modern Western political history.

To summarize, the prevalence of different non-elite orientations toward the social and political world varies with changes in the sizes and situations of the three basic work force components as societies pass through the four development levels. In conjunction with our summary of the work force configuration that characterizes each development level (see p. 25), the historical variation in non-elite orientations between the four levels can be illustrated as follows:

Level 1	*Level 2*	*Level 3*	*Level 4*
prevailingly egalitarian	prevailingly egalitarian	egalitarian – ¼ managerial – ¼ inconsistent – ½	prevailingly managerial

The importance of this variation is that it limits major political options as societies pass through the development sequence. Seriously egalitarian regimes are possible, although very rare, only in Levels 1 and 2. The revolutions that occasionally bring them into power, even if only for brief periods, are impossible in Levels 3 and 4, although, as in Cuba, egalitarian factions masquerading as reformists may win power in organized warfare. Populistic conservative or fascist regimes enjoying wide popular support cannot exist in Levels 1 and 2, but they have been real possibilities in Level 3. Except where subnational cultural and regional conflicts intervene, political conflicts in Levels 1, 2 and 3 necessarily have a strong social class basis. However, this is not the case in Level 4 societies because their pervasive bureaucratic cultures blur social classes and create more pressing conflicts across class lines between elites, insiders and outsiders.

III

Despite the substantial uniformity of non-elite limits on major political options as societies develop, the intensity and consequences of political conflict vary considerably between societies located in the same development levels. This variation is associated primarily with the character of elites. Four different kinds of elites can exist in all or some of Levels 2, 3 and 4. Accordingly, the kind of elite that actually exists in a given society is only partly determined by the development level at which that society is located. Instead, the kind of elite that exists has been determined mainly by the occurrence or non-occurrence or particular types of rather rare historical events. These events cannot be predicted from a knowledge of non-elite configurations and orientations, that is, from the level of development attained.

Before distinguishing the four kinds of elites that can exist in the several development levels, however, it is necessary to consider what all elites have in common. This involves noticing the difference between the situations of ruling groups in most Level 1 societies and those of ruling groups in all more developed societies.

Although history records scattered, highly local cases of fairly egalitarian societies in Level 1, such as some of the New England colonies in North America during the seventeenth century and some of the Swiss cantons before and during the eighteenth and early nineteenth centuries, societies with sharp class divisions have been overwhelmingly more frequent in Level 1. This is because these societies have usually been dominated by leisured aristocracies whose members were better armed, better informed, better motivated, and free of working tasks. Membership in these aristocracies extended only to defined family lines, and most aristocrats took very nearly whatever measures they were inclined to take in order to keep the lower classes intimidated. In cases of serious unrest, aristocracies commonly took action in much the same way as they went hunting. Ordinarily, they prevailed. Only a few Level 1 societies remotely located across oceans, behind swamps, or up mountains succeeded in keeping out, or in driving out, aristocrats.

There has been a misleading but very widespread tendency to generalize from the existence of aristocratic ruling classes in Level 1 societies to conditions of rulership in more developed societies. This has been misleading because it conceals the real source of power in conditions of greater socio-economic development. In all societies above Level 1, power belongs to persons who are strategically placed in bureaucratic structures. Such persons naturally have families and personal entourages whose members derive substantial advantages from their close attachments to the bureaucratically influential. But, strictly speaking, these advantages are derivative. That is, they are not the same the privileged statuses of family members in Level 1 aristocracies who, for the most part, ensured their own dominance and advantages by more or less spontaneous activities.

In more developed societies it is therefore misleading to conceive of a ruling class of privileged families because privilege and power emanate not from the family itself, but from the strategic positions which one or more of its members happen to hold in complex bureaucracies. Obviously, there is always some amount of stratification according to family membership and cronyism, even in cultures whose principles avowedly oppose it. In Washington, in Moscow, in Belgrade or in Buenos Aires there are strategically placed elite persons (ministers, directors, legislators, managers, military commanders) and their families and associates who have a good deal more to do with what happens politically than does the ordinary person. But these groupings do not form ruling classes in the historic sense. Rather, they comprise elites and their hangers-on.

Because this distinction between the bureaucratic basis of elites and the family and property bases of ruling classes is the subject of great confusion, it requires further elaboration. The operations of all sizeable organizations, from military units to universities, involve regular allocation and reallocation of tasks, and therefore of their members' statuses. For such organizations to function, decisions that transcend individual interests must constantly be taken. Yet there can rarely be any firm consensus among organizational members about the content of these decisions. This is partly because in any organization at any given time few persons can be in the positions that afford views of its total effort. It is also because the necessity for constant decisions deprives most organizational members of the time they would need to work out their common interest in specific alternatives, supposing this could be done at all. In addition, because even minor day-to-day personnel and housekeeping decisions change organizational structures and requirements, members' alignments and their conceptions of common interests are also constantly changing. Any developing consensus in detailed matters therefore always lags behind the current organizational situation and is more or less irrelevant to it.

These difficulties make organizational structures and processes inherently arbitrary in character. They are created and modified by persons who happen to be in strategic decision-making locations at any moment, although these persons can never convincingly demonstrate to all participants the correctness of their decisions and actions. Yet, in order for large, bureaucratized organizations to function, someone must decide.

It is essential in this situation that those who happen to be strategically located have the power to enforce their decisions. This requires communications systems through which decisions flow from those who make them to those who implement them, and systems of rewards and punishments to ensure that these decisions are obeyed. In short, there must be hierarchies of power in all large and complex organizations. If we call the persons who command these hierarchies elites, then we can say that organization beyond some minimum size and complexity necessarily creates elites. Furthermore, because such organizations are themselves concentrations of power in the wider society, those who command them normally have disproportionate societal power and influence. It is in this sense that elites are an inherent feature of all societies in which there are large bureaucratic organizations, that is, all Level 2, 3 and 4 societies.

Located in strategic bureaucratic positions, and limited by the many conflicting organizational pressures that routinely impinge on such positions, elites lack the power to follow their own inclinations with little or no disguise and subterfuge. To a substantial extent, this distinguishes them from the aristocrats commonly found in Level 1 societies. While the classic elitist paradigm seemed to assume that elites could act in this completely unrestricted way, our paradigm does not. Although elites have the important advantages of more time, more information, and more opportunities to concert their actions, they must always seek non-elite support within the limits of what non-elite orientations at the different development levels allow.

Strictly speaking, therefore, all that can be generally said about the common situation of elites is that by shrewd and informed action elite persons are ordinarily able to preserve their influential positions over a considerable period of years. Sometimes they arrange quietly to retire to comfortable obscurity. Sometimes they raise themselves to greater power and influence. Not infrequently their careers end in disaster. Normally, merely retaining their bureaucratic positions requires elites to choose within narrow ranges of policies, and normally they voluntarily choose to operate within these limits.

IV

Persons who hold strategically influential positions in large and powerful organizations are usually highly distrustful of each other. This common situation describes a *disunified elite*. Its members form cliques, factions and broader alliances in order to fight each other ruthlessly for careerist and partisan advantages. When this happens in Level 2 societies, as it usually does at that level, the most entrenched elite factions, the 'conservatives', seek non-elite support obliquely by appealing to religious beliefs or ethnic prejudices, and they follow policies aimed at maintaining the *status quo* as regards their own, usually landed, possessions and bureaucratic supremacy. Less well entrenched elites, such as bourgeois position-holders and many professionals, including teachers and journalists, frequently invoke egalitarian principles in order to gain non-elite support. This was typical of the leaders who styled themselves 'liberals' in eighteenth- and nineteenth-century France and in nineteenth-century Spain and Latin America. Given the prevailingly egalitarian orientation of non-elites in Level 2, this kind of elite conflict can occasionally lead to a temporary, revolutionary collapse of bureaucratic power and the status order, as in France in 1792. Such an outcome involves the killing and displacement of many elite persons.

Similarly, in Level 3 societies different factions in a disunified elite make strong appeals to the egalitarian and to the anti-egalitarian bodies of non-elites. But because of the predominance of an anti-egalitarian orientation among non-elites in Level 3, the former appeals never result in successful levelling revolutions. However, appeals to anti-egalitarian forces sometimes eventuate in fascist or right-wing dictatorships of a highly repressive character, as in Chile after 1973. When this happens, those elites who have appealed to egalitarian sentiments are usually excluded from all strategic positions. Frequently, they are driven underground or killed.

Levelling or fascist revolutions as a result of elite disunity in Levels 2 and 3 are unusual outcomes, however. Much more often, elite disunity in these levels is manifested merely in continuing political instability. That is, where elites are disunified power normally passes irregularly from one elite faction to another through *coups d'état* or simple rebellions which the military and police refuse to suppress. This kind of instability is readily observable in the politics of many European countries over recent centuries, in nearly all Latin American countries since their independence, and in most African, Middle Eastern and Asian countries during their post-colonial histories.

Thus disunity is easily the most common condition of elites the world over. In a significant number of societies, however, elites give the appearance of much higher degrees of trust and co-operation. These may be called 'unified' elites, and they are of two distinct kinds: *ideological unified* and *consensual unified*. The former arise out of the leaderships of tightly organized and ideologically defined political movements when these manage to displace all the persons who have previously held strategically influential positions. This can occur through military victories in warfare, with or without the intervention of foreign powers, as in Eastern Europe, China, North Korea, and Cuba during the period following World War II. Or it can occur in Level 2 societies through a levelling revolution, such as Brinton described, from which a tightly disciplined movement with an ostensibly egalitarian ideology emerges as the sole holder of power, as in Russia in 1921. It can also occur in Level 3 societies when movements with a populistic, anti-egalitarian ideology come to power by the mere surrender of a large part of the pre-existing elite, as in Italy between 1922 and 1926 and Germany in 1933.

As is ordinarily true with a disunified elite, the ideological unified elite, once established, appears to perpetuate itself indefinitely in Levels 2 and 3 unless it is defeated in international warfare. But unlike those accompanying a disunified elite, the political institutions through which an ideological unified elite rules are stable, and *coups d'état* and other irregular seizures of governing power do not occur. This is because the ideological unified elite severely penalizes dissent from the single ideology it espouses and from the way the central bureaucratic authority is currently applying that ideology to policy questions.

The other kind of unified elite, the consensual unified elite, does not depend on a sharply defined ideological commitment and the systematic use of it to regulate the positions that may be expressed publicly. Its unity exists *de facto* in the failure of elite persons to organize and accentuate opposing non-elite orientations. Historically, this has been most apparent in some Level 2 and Level 3 societies where elites clearly refused to inflame the highly volatile egalitarian and anti-egalitarian orientations of non-elites. This leads one to suppose that rival elite persons in this kind of elite voluntarily moderate their quarrels and rivalries. As a consequence, political conflicts tend to be moderate, and there is little evidence that elite persons seriously expect to be penalized or ruined if they end up on the losing side in a conflict. It follows that where such elites exist, political institutions are stable and immune to the simpler and cruder forms of power seizures that are characteristic of disunified elites.

The inclination of persons in a consensual unified elite to take publicly opposed positions while continuing to respect and support established institutions and procedures makes this kind of elite compatible with a fairly wide degree of representative democratic politics. A key feature of consensual unified elites, in other words, is their ability to shape and contain issues whose open and dogmatic expression would create disastrous conflict. This and this alone makes representative political institutions that are guided by reasonably competitive and influential elections possible, although not inevitable. It is in this sense that a consensual unified elite may be said to be a precondition of a practical degree of democratic politics, a point to which we shall return in succeeding chapters.

Consensual unified elites have mainly arisen among the leaderships of largely self-governing colonies or dependencies at the times they gained full independence. In such cases, the native elites united in opposition to the exercise of serious power by agents of the imperial country. When this limited outside authority was brought to an end, the unified condition of the native elite, which now became the sole elite, persisted. In this way, consensual unified elites got started in the Netherlands, the United States, and in such former British dominions as Canada, Australia and New Zealand.

However, in three very important historical instances, leaders representing factions in previously disunified elites apparently bargained out arrangements for the future that eliminated mutual distrust and produced elite consensus and unity. The instances were England in 1688–9, Sweden in 1809 and Mexico in 1933. All three societies were in Level 2 at the time. It may therefore be doubted whether disunified elites in Levels 3 or 4 would be small enough and sufficiently free of control by their diverse non-elite supporters to arrange strictly similar settlements. Except for one possibility considered below, however, these are the only known origins of consensual unified elites. Because the relevant colonial or Level 2 circumstances in which they originated historically are largely absent in the contemporary world, it may be illusory to expect that the representative democratic politics associated with consensual unified elites will find a much wider global application in the future than it has at present.

The kinds of elites sketched to this point may be summarized. In Level 2 and Level 3 societies an elite may be disunified with the consequence that political institutions are unstable, or it may be unified, ideologically or consensually, with the consequence that political institutions are stable. With one recent exception, that of France from about 1970, all the societies that have so far reached Level 4 have done so with consensual unified elites and, consequently, stable institutions. However, the historical experience with Level 4 must be judged too brief to allow us to say whether disunified or ideologically unified elites are compatible with this development level.

Disunified elites represent an original elite condition, which first occurs in divisions within aristocracies and between them and emerging non-elite leadership groupings in Level 1 societies. As societies progress from Level 1 to Levels 2 and 3, opposing non-elite orientations are ready sources of support for the efforts of disunified elite factions to displace each other. On rare occasions this seesawing struggle can open the way to events in which a tightly knit ideological movement manages to substitute itself for the previously dominant elites. Thus ideological unified elites arise from victories in socialist or fascist revolutions, or in international warfare. A consensual unified elite arises out of independence movements in dependent territories that have already been largely self-governing or, very rarely, through more or less negotiated settlements of differences between the main factions in a previously disunified elite.

With only two qualifications, both kinds of unified elites seem to be reliably self-perpetuating in Levels 2 and 3 regardless of non-elite configurations, and this is possibly true of these elites in Level 4 societies as well. One qualification is that incursions by foreign military forces can, of course, displace any kind of elite. The other qualification is that the presence of a unified elite is not a completely effective barrier to the breakup of a society as a result of subnational geographic cleavages. If different regions develop consistently different values and interests, a unified elite might break up into warring parts like the society as a whole, or it might become disunified in the forcible attempt to bring back the seceding regions. But subject to the outcomes of international or organized civil warfare or secessionary tendencies, elite unity seems to persist in Levels 2, 3 and 4 once it is created.

In addition to the rare negotiated settlements within disunified elites and the unifying effects of independence struggles in self-governing colonies, there is one other way in which consensual unified elites have been created. This involves the evolution of a disunified elite into an 'imperfectly unified' one in a Level 3 society, and then the development of a fully consensual unified elite at about the time when this society reaches Level 4.

An *imperfectly unified elite* consists of two main factions that correspond to the egalitarian and anti-egalitarian components of non-elites in Level 3. It arises only after the anti-egalitarian elite faction clearly demonstrates through elections and other forms of representative politics that it has the support of a reliable and clear-cut anti-egalitarian majority among non-elites. By demonstrating that it can apparently count on continuously holding office merely through elections, the anti-egalitarian elite faction takes on the appearance of being a 'permanent government'. Because of their association with the minority, egalitarian component of non-elites, the rest of the elite find themselves apparently permanently excluded from top political office.

Over a generation or so, and occasionally – as in Belgium – over a longer period, this situation can foster fairly stable political institutions. The anti-egalitarian elite faction's seemingly permanent hold on government through mere democratic elections and procedures gradually reduces the readiness of military or bureaucratic factions to resort to *coups d'état* in order to stave off egalitarian victories. At the same time, the egalitarian elite and non-elite forces are powerless to upset this situation by either democratic or revolutionary means. However, their frustration is such that vehement demonstrations and riots to protest against antiegalitarian policies are frequent. These give the regimes operated by imperfectly unified elites a much more unstable appearance than those operated by consensual unified elites. But it is frequently clear over longer periods that such demonstrations of discontent are insufficient to overturn existing institutions. Typical cases of regimes produced by imperfectly unified elites are Japan since the end of Allied occupation in 1955, Belgium through most of its history as a nation-state down to 1960, Italy during nearly the entire post-war period, and France under the Gaullist and post-Gaullist regimes of the 1960s and 1970s.

An imperfectly unified elite thus occupies an intermediate position between a disunified elite and a consensual unified one in our paradigm. It is not, however, as reliably self-perpetuating as either disunified or unified elites are. Probably it can avoid reverting to disunity only if substantial economic stability, or even growth, is present. This prevents the dissidence of the egalitarian elite faction from reaching a level that is incompatible with stable, representative government. Where economic conditions are deteriorating, however, the outbreak of violent egalitarian movements may force the imposition of military dictatorship and thus a return to elite disunity. This was the significance of the Tupamaro movement and its forcible repression by the military in Uruguay during 1973. On the other hand, if an imperfectly unified elite can persist until the close approach of Level 4, the egalitarian elite faction may acknowledge the dominant non-elite orientation by moderating its egalitarian appeals sufficiently to become a serious candidate for majority support. When and if this happens, the elite becomes consensual unified as occurred in Denmark and Norway during the 1930s and as may now be occurring in France, Italy and Japan.[4]

Description of this third way in which consensual unified elites have originated completes our paradigmatic treatment of the origins, characteristics, transformations and political consequences of the four kinds of elites that have existed during socioeconomic development to date. Within the limits of a brief presentation, we have tried to notice the extremely diverse' and complex national (and international) circumstances in which each kind of elite has been embedded historically. This has required a number of complicated generalizations utilizing somewhat unfamiliar terms and concepts. However, it is also possible to portray our paradigmatic elite variations in a more simplified, schematic way, and this is attempted in Figure 2·1.

If a three-dimensional schematic portrayal of the full elite and non-elite paradigm were possible, then Figure 1 would be 'superimposed' on our diagrams of the non-elite configurations and orientations that characterize each development level (see pp. 25 and 31). This superimposition would suggest the dynamic way in which non-elite variation limits elite variation at each level, as well as the way in which elites nevertheless vary independently of non-elites as shown in Figure 2·1.

It will be seen that Figure 2·1's depiction of elites in Level 4 societies contains several question marks. Because experience with Level 4 societies is as yet very limited, this is the most speculative part of our paradigm. With the possible exception of France (Level 4 from about 1970 with an elite that may still be imperfectly unified), elites in all Level 4 societies are currently of the consensual unified kind. One question is whether they will be able to perpetuate themselves by successfully managing the novel conflicts that arise in Level 4. The fact that consensual unified elites have always done so in Level 2 and Level 3 societies does not mean that they can certainly do so in Level 4 societies because the character of non-elite conflict is greatly altered in Level 4.

A second question is whether societies with disunified elites or only recently acquired imperfectly unified ones can reach Level 4

---

4 Elsewhere, we have discussed the prospects for a full unification of imperfectly unified elites in France and Italy; see G. L. Field and J. Higley, 'Imperfectly unified elites: the cases of France and Italy', in R. Tomasson (ed.), *Comparative Studies in Sociology*, New York, JAI Press, 1978, pp. 295–317.

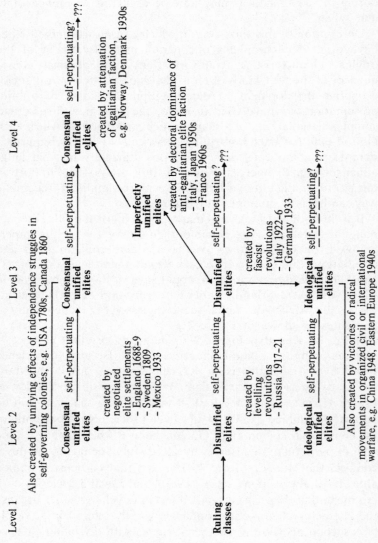

Figure 2·1   Variations in elite types during socioeconomic development

at all. If they can, will the novel conflicts in Level 4 quickly prove unmanageable for such elites? If so, will this trigger negative development and widespread disorder or a further unification of the elite? Third, can societies with ideological unified elites reach Level 4, and if they can will Level 4 conflicts change those elites? The seriousness of this last question is indicated by the experience of Czechoslovakia during 1967 and 1968, even though the Czech case's outcome was determined by Russian military intervention.

These possibilities must be treated strictly as undetermined. Their outcomes depend on elite behaviour that cannot as yet be foreseen. However, the success of consensual unified elites in maintaining stable institutions at the lower development levels suggests that they may be as successful at Level 4. In subsequent chapters we shall discuss the kinds of elite attitudes and actions that seem to be required to manage non-elite conflicts in Level 4, as well as to manage the relations between Level 4 societies and the many societies that are temporarily or permanently located at lower development levels. To set the stage for these considerations, however, it is necessary to examine non-elite orientations in Level 4 societies in greater detail.

V

After a brief initial period of elite complacency and non-elite preoccupation with spreading affluence, conflicts that are both ominous and possibly intractable begin to emerge in Level 4 societies.[5] There is first the 'insider–outsider' conflict already alluded to. This arises because advanced technology eliminates a strict, demonstrable need for human labour that is great enough to keep a large proportion of non-elites steadily employed. Increasingly, the production of material objects is seen to be retarded by the retention of human labour instead of introducing automated processes. Food, clothing and most material objects are produced in quantities that are more than sufficient to meet

5 Elsewhere, we have detailed the general characteristics of this initial 'halcyon' stage of Level 4 societies, and we have described their manifestations in Norway during the 1960s. See G. L. Field and J. Higley, *Elites in Developed Societies: Theoretical Reflections on an Initial Stage in Norway*, Beverly Hills; SAGE Professional Papers in Comparative Politics, 1972; and J. Higley, G. L. Field and K. Grøholt, op. cit., pp. 271–335.

the needs and desires of a large part of the population, although minorities of unemployed or underemployed persons with little disposable income continue to live in relative poverty. Overall, however, the demand for more material goods is at most weak and artificially stimulated.

To some extent the non-elites displaced from agricultural and industrial production by advanced technology are absorbed into a variety of service activities. Contrary to expectations during the initial stage of Level 4, however, this absorption cannot keep up with the work force redundancies created in the primary and secondary sectors because, beyond certain low limits and costs, the demand for more services is also weak and artificially stimulated. This problem is further seriously aggravated by changes in family structure and values that result in the entrance of many women into the labour market.

The resulting high levels of unemployment and underemployment are not spread evenly or randomly through all categories of non-elites in Level 4 societies. They are concentrated among youth, among deprived minority groups, and among women. Initially, lack of skills combined with occupationally inappropriate temperamental or attitudinal dispositions account for these unemployment concentrations. With their inevitable lack of experience, youth are less suitable for the subtle bargaining and give and take that characterize many service jobs. In addition, many youth come from culturally deprived minority groups, and they lack the verbal and social skills generally present in the rest of the population. Many youth also come from backgrounds that have been sufficiently comfortable to create expectations about having really interesting and responsible work. But nowhere nearly enough such jobs are available or apparently needed. Entering the work force *en masse,* women encounter the need for very different attitudes than were customarily transmitted among their sex when they were brought up to expect strictly specialized occupational or subordinate family roles.

For these reasons, youth, members of deprived minority groups, and women confront real difficulties in staying in the work force. When few jobs are available anyway, these groups are much less likely to get them. Naturally, they resent the greater incidence of unemployment, underemployment, and insecure employment among their ranks. It only takes a short time for these resentments to become translated into anti-social attitudes and behaviour. This is especially the case where history has left distinct, culturally deprived categories. Once this happens, it is more difficult than ever to absorb these non-elites into the work force because they tend to want more desirable jobs than employers assess them as competent to perform.

It is unclear what elites can do to mediate and curtail this conflict. Unless a great decline in current levels of affluence occurs, mere economic measures designed to increase the need for, or the profitability of, employment, for instance by reducing payroll and other taxes on employers or by limiting unemployment and welfare payments to workers, are unlikely to have favourable effects. One of the overriding dangers facing Level 4 societies is therefore the tendency toward the growth of alienated groupings who are motivated more and more by desires for retaliation and revenge against a society that has pushed them to the outside.

The second major conflict in Level 4 is that between elites and insiders. This arises from the sharp increase in populistic and seemingly egalitarian attitudes among non-elites who appear to be reasonably integrated into the job market and who therefore do not experience the basically alienating circumstances of outsiders. Somewhat ironically, these attitudes are initially most clearly articulated by relatively small categories of the best-off and best-educated non-elites. The irony dissolves, however, when it is recognized that this is, in fact, a means by which these persons increase their power and influence.

Possibly because of their freer and less restrained upbringings, the well-off and educated non-elite cadres of Level 4 societies are especially unsympathetic to bureaucratic decisions whose rationales are either not understood or rejected. After all, a main feature of childhood and adolescent learning in affluent families and suburbs is the injunction to question and to demand plausible explanations for decisions that result in deprivations. In any event, there occurs a great increase in 'participation' in decision-making in Level 4 societies, mainly at relatively high bureaucratic and social levels. Many kinds of decisions that in the past were made by elite persons without need for explanation become subject to processes that are designed to maximize input from interested parties of all sorts, including fellow workers.

While formal decision-making power is seldom actually transferred to participating groups, it becomes more and more difficult to take decisions to which large numbers of interested parties object. This could be seen as a thoroughly harmless, even healthy development except that many decisions, especially in their details, are not capable of being rationalized to the satisfaction of all concerned in large-scale organizations. Decisions are necessary in the first place because of limited resources or because established allocations of resources are having conflicting effects. Inevitably, any decision that can be made will disadvantage some substantial and articulate grouping. Given this, it is usually impossible to demonstrate clearly to the satisfaction of all, or even most, participants that one decision is better than another. In reality, of course, many decisions are inherently arbitrary, and yet such arbitrary decisions are probably necessary to keep an organization functioning.

Most experienced and sophisticated bureaucratic personnel probably recognize, or at least suspect, these unpleasant facts of life in large-scale organizations. Yet no one wishes to accept an arbitrary decision if it adversely affects him or those he sympathizes with, and if there are ways of stopping it. The trend toward openness and greater participation in decision-making, which can readily be justified ideologically in terms of goal values like freedom and equality, thus threatens to deprive elites of power to make what in many cases may be essential decisions. Here too it is unclear how elites can mediate and curtail this growing conflict. In this respect, a second overriding danger in Level 4 societies is the tendency toward substantial elite, and therefore organizational, paralysis.

VI

What is the basic utility of this restated paradigm? While we shall address this question in greater detail in chapter 6, it may not be out of place to summarize its main uses here.

First, the restated paradigm suggests a cogent explanation of at least one key aspect of modern societies that has previously not had any accepted or cogent explanation. This is the stability of political institutions that has clearly distinguished some modern societies from all others. Violence, usurpation, assassination, and in recent decades military *coups d'état* are commonplace in the high politics of most societies for which there are recorded histories. Yet there have been a few 'republican' regimes, such as

Great Britain after 1689, the United States from its inception, and a handful of others, in which power has been transmitted peacefully by elections or other institutional means over long periods, and in which instabilities of the usual kinds are not taken as serious possibilities. The restated paradigm explains this by focusing on elite unity and disunity, and by showing that these phenomena are not explicable in terms of variations in non-elites.

On this basis, the paradigm also reasons less certainly, but suggestively, about various other features of politics in nation-states. It does this by conceiving of non-elite orientations at different development levels as comprising arenas for elite action. The non-elite orientations which comprise these arenas need to be considered, acceded to in part, and ignored or compromised in part by the few incumbents of strategic positions from which serious political decisions can be taken and enforced. The paradigm holds that the essential choices of politics are elite choices because non-elite orientations are fairly firmly fixed by the basic circumstances of different kinds of work in the four levels of development.

In these and numerous other respects, the paradigm is fundamentally at odds with utopian viewpoints which assume that basic changes in human nature, orientations, and values can be brought about by argument, schooling, or by deliberately rearranged socialization processes of a wider sort. In terms of values, the elitist paradigm only allows for greater or lesser degrees of humaneness and generosity to be distributed in greater or lesser proportions within a population. And it sees greater humaneness and generosity as depending mainly on the successful management of potential conflicts among non-elites by elites.

If one accepts that these limitations in choice and action are imposed by reality and are not merely the perverse predispositions of the authors, then one may proceed with this restated paradigm to a substantially greater understanding of politics than is possible under the one-sided Marxist and classical elitist paradigms, the indeterminate democratic paradigm, or the trivial welfare statist paradigm.

Chapter 3
Elitism and liberalism

At the beginning of this century, personal safety and respectful treatment in most of life's contingencies were assured to members of upper- and middle-class families in Western Europe, the countries settled by English-speaking people, and probably in most of the larger cities of Latin America, Africa and Southern Asia. This was generally true even for most upper- and middle-class persons without European ancestors, although the privileges of Europeans in colonial areas were embarrassing and humiliating to arrived 'native' families. Between the well-behaved, the well-dressed and the well-spoken in all these areas, at least, Western liberal conceptions of personal dignity and impartial justice were generally professed and practised.

In 1900, of course, such treatment did not extend reliably to members of lower-class families, ethnic minorities and women acting outside conventional roles. Especially in countries not directly influenced by British practices and especially when they asserted rights that dominant interests did not think they had, persons in lower statuses were not reliably respected. There is no reason to suppose, however, that they were any less respected or any less safe from abuses than such persons have been throughout history. On the contrary, the widespread profession of liberal values among well-off strata probably resulted in the respectful treatment of many of these persons in particular circumstances. On the whole, in other words, much larger proportions of populations in 1900 were accorded respect by authorities and institutions than ever before in complex societies. This meant, in turn, that larger proportions of populations than ever before lived lives of personal self-respect.

In 1900 governments in Western Europe and in the countries settled by English-speaking people derived much of their legitimacy from public elections of representative assemblies. To be sure, monarchies in Germany and Sweden claimed a significant degree of independent power, and monarchies in Spain and Portugal appeared to have such power. Nevertheless, the liberal notion of political choices in real party contests by at least moderately large electorates was the prevailing standard of political authority, and in most of these countries there was no expectation that military *coups* were likely to upset these choices. Although liberal political practices did not extend much beyond the English-speaking countries and Western Europe, representative government tended to be accepted by political activists as the preferred model in most other areas of the globe. In part, of course, this reflected Western imperial power. But whatever the cause, except for some aspects of German political thought, liberal political principles seemed intellectually dominant, and liberal practices increasingly ascendant, throughout the world in 1900.

In retrospect, the period around 1900 seems to have been the high water mark in liberalism's advance. Between then and now the area of liberal rule in the world has not expanded significantly, and serious interruptions of liberal practices have occurred in many of the countries in which they seemed increasingly influential in 1900. Austria, Belgium, Denmark, France, Germany, Italy, the Netherlands, Norway, Portugal and Spain all experienced the suppression of liberal practices for substantial periods before, during, or after World War II. Moreover, Russia since 1917, and a number of other countries since 1945–50, have professed communist principles which in practice disregard the personal rights involved in liberalism and eschew meaningful electoral contests and choices. In 1980, if one notes that Germany is divided, and if one takes the intentions of the current Spanish and Portuguese regimes for attainments, it is barely possible to say that the area of liberal rule is about what it was in 1900.

Unlike 1900, however, no Western liberal country today exerts much political influence and power outside this area except, as far as raw power goes, the United States. The moral acceptability of liberal principles and practices outside the West seems dubious at best. It is no longer the case, for example, that members of upper- and middle-class families are assured of safety and respectful treatment in the cities of Latin America, Africa, the Middle East and Southern Asia. In these areas, politics are now explosively dangerous. In the face of political kidnapping on a scale largely unknown since the European Middle Ages, the safety, personal liberty and self-respect of educated, wealthy and politically prominent persons are now frequently at risk. As it was historically before the appearance of liberal and semi-liberal states, politics in much of the world has again become a dangerous but unavoidable activity that tends to degrade, humiliate, and sometimes destroy all but the most fortunate of those who engage in it.

Even Western liberal states are no longer exempt from terrorist political acts and the taking of hostages. In countries that only recently were very secure, upper-class and otherwise prominent and influential persons can no longer count on personal safety and respectful treatment. Wherever they move, they face the real, if statistically still remote, possiblity of being killed, maimed, or held hostage in the interest of some often obscure political sect's public relations efforts. This circumstance tends, of course, to destroy liberal attitudes among those who are threatened.

Under the elitist paradigm, the immediate reason for the failure of liberal practices to spread beyond the comparatively few countries which already enjoyed them at the beginning of this century is clear. This is the necessity for a consensual unified elite before any stable pattern of government involving substantial personal freedom and meaningful electoral choice can be established. In 1900 consensual unified elites existed in Great Britain, the United States, the Netherlands, Sweden and Switzerland. Canada, Australia and New Zealand had formed or were forming such elites in the process of sloughing off the last significant British controls over them. Several other European countries – Norway, Denmark and Belgium – had imperfectly unified elites. Moreover, some countries with disunified elites, such as Spain, Portugal, France, Germany and Austria, were attempting to operate representative political institutions, and they showed some respect for personal liberties.

In nearly all Latin American, and, in so far as they were independent, Southern Asian, Middle Eastern and African countries, however, consensual unified or even imperfectly unified elites did not exist in 1900. Unfortunately, both then and subsequently Western liberals failed to recognize this important structural difference. Instead, they increasingly urged on these countries democratic suffrage, respect for personal liberties, and various constitutional reforms on the mistaken assumption that by such measures countries could move directly from unstable and illiberal regimes to stable and liberal ones. This failure of liberal thinking to understand the elitist character of legally and constitutionally established representative government was largely responsible for liberalism's failure to expand its effective influence in the world after 1900. In the absence of any real understanding of the pre-conditions for liberal regimes, only the most unlikely run of luck could have expanded liberal influence beyond the area that it already dominated in 1900.

The blind spots in liberal thought also affected political trends in Western countries themselves. In particular, a marked tendency to avoid unpleasant assumptions about the ultimate nature of political societies, and a general neglect of values as such, led to the basically mistaken welfare statist notions that are now intel-lectually dominant in these societies. Motivated by these notions, as we argued in chapter 1, persons who think of themselves as liberals have increasingly failed to do what would achieve liberal goals, and at the same time they have done many things which are irrelevant or actually harmful to these goals.

In this chapter, therefore, we shall try to identify where and why the evolution of liberal thought miscarried. We think the most basic problem has been the unwillingness of well-off and conscientious persons in Western societies to recognize the essen-tially elitist character of their circumstances and interests. In other words, a general failure to consider the complementarity of elitist and liberal principles has been at the heart of a serious doctrinal degeneration within liberalism. The most important practical aspect of this degeneration has been the relation of democratic and other egalitarian values to liberal values. Although democracy and other forms of equality obviously belong among the ideal goals of any liberal political system, they are not, contrary to the assumptions commonly made by liberals, reliable instruments for promoting the political liberalization of societies.

I

The degeneration of liberal doctrine during this century has been rooted in the unwillingness of liberals to accept certain basic assumptions about the political nature of human society. Thus liberals have been extremely reluctant to assume that politics arises out of, and only out of, rationally irreconcilable conflicts of interest among people. Such conflicts are irreconcilable in the sense that the parties to them cannot be shown or persuaded that they are mistaken about their interests. Not all conflicts have this character, of course, but many do, and it is these that are the basis of politics.

Where conflicts of interest are not rationally reconcilable, politics is the alternative to warfare. As history readily shows, it is hardly a reliable alternative, yet it is very widely and frequently chosen. This is because the many people in any society who lack substantial self-confidence, ambition and assertiveness are usually prepared to tolerate politics in order to reduce the amount of violence and disorder that would otherwise occur. They are prepared to put up with political actions that are unsatisfactory to themselves in order to create some semblance of peace. Behind any smoothly functioning political system, in other words, are the tacit, expediential conclusions of individuals and groups that trying to claim all they think they deserve is unprofitable, and that conforming to the political organization and the distribution of privilege that happen to exist offers a better return than they might obtain by openly challenging the established order.

Because the conflicts that give rise to politics are not rationally reconcilable, political actions can never fully 'solve' social problems in any objective moral sense. 'Social justice' can never be attained through politics (nor through any other activity) because in assuming that all differences of interest are ultimately mistaken it is an empty concept. At most, political actions result only in 'settlements' which contain, discourage or repress the expression of interests that are not, and for the most part could not be, fully satisfied.[1]

While political settlements usually involve fairly even-handed compromises between entrenched groupings, they necessarily sacrifice some interests that happen not to be so well represented at the points where decisions are reached. One reason for this is that persons who engage in politics actively, and who are in positions to take decisions, normally expect to gain something for themselves and their friends from their political activities. Thus, in any settlement some interests are sacrificed merely by politicians' efforts to ensure that they, at least, are not disadvantaged by it.

Because there are no strictly objective moral solutions to many conflicts of interest, and because those who make their weight felt

1 We derive this distinction and the terms for its expression from Bertrand de Jouvenel. See his *The Pure Theory of Politics*, Yale University Press, 1963.

in determining political settlements regularly produce more advantages for themselves and their allies than for others, politicians are commonly thought to be immoral, callous and deceitful. From the perspectives that would be appropriate in judging many non-political activities, they are. But as a generalization about most or all politicians, this common judgment is erroneous because politics is a necessary activity that does not allow fully open and trusting behaviour. Political action that is naively open and trusting is normally ineffective, while action that does not seek to coerce some persons in ways that are advantageous to others is by definition not political.

Given this nature of politics *per se,* the moral judgments *properly* appropriate to it are much more complex, subtle and controversial. They are concerned with effectiveness, with humaneness, and with culturally limited notions of fairness. Basically, they are concerned with the obligation of politicians to avoid practices that *unnecessarily* reduce the satisfaction of some persons or *unnecessarily* degrade persons' attitudes and behaviour. Inevitably, these standards are culture-bound to a degree. For instance, liberals, as we shall specify later, seek political practices that would create or preserve a certain type of personality which they prefer. The political practices of socialists, on the other hand, are chosen with a view to fostering a somewhat different kind of personality. This means that liberals and socialists will, to some extent, disagree about what constitutes unnecessarily harsh and degrading political practices.

The social function of politics is to make possible the existence of all larger territorial organizations of people. These range from city-states to modern nation-states to world empires to weakly organized and only somewhat pacified supranational areas such as the European Economic Community or the United Nations. But when politics successfully perform this function by suppressing overt conflict and producing a reliability of expectations in social life, they tend to conceal their own nature from the persons who benefit most from such political success. Secure and influential, these persons lose sight of the basis and function of politics, and they increasingly mistake their own situations and sensibilities for those of people in general. They find it almost impossible to believe, for example, that the political institutions and processes that so effectively protect and nurture them are seen as more or

less iniquitous by less fortunate people in their own society and
in other societies.

In this way, a really successful political system tends to undermine its own basis. The most favoured strata in it come to contain
larger and larger numbers of sentimental and unrealistic persons.
These individuals like to talk of such things as social justice,
management by consensus, politics without coercion, conflict reso-
lution and other constructs that can only be mainly imaginary. To
a degree, they impose respect for such constructs on the politicians
who need their support. This phenomenon can be seen clearly in
the naive ideal of Colonel House, President Wilson's negotiator
and friend, to the effect that nations should be expected to behave
toward each other according to the same morality as governs, or
is supposed to govern, individual persons within a civilized
society.[2]

When it comes to be widely professed, such naiveté cripples the
effectiveness of politicians. In the eyes of less advantaged people
at home and abroad, such professions are patently insincere, and
the politicians and other spokesmen who express them become
contemptible. Only a ruthless tradition of intellectual honesty, or
a protected private tradition of objectivity among elites and their
immediate supporters can resist the tendency of successful politics
to undermine its own basis. The politics of Western liberal countries at the beginning of this century was perhaps the most effective politics ever practised. Yet, the intellectual life of none of
these countries was able to prevent the naive moral claims that
this success inspired from coming to pervade the thought and
utterances of many otherwise sophisticated citizens.

II

Liberalism's doctrinal degeneration has been closely related to the
problem of discriminating between fact and value propositions
that has been so central to this century's intellectual life. The

---

2 'I endeavoured to point out that we could not get very far toward a proper
  international understanding until one nation treated another as individuals
  treat one another' (Colonel House, quoted by Patrick Devlin, *Too Proud to
  Fight: Woodrow Wilson's Neutrality*, Oxford University Press, 1975). Perhaps
  the earliest public figure to whom one can impute the equating of public and
  private morality was Gladstone; see ibid., p. 125.

effort to clarify traditional philosophy's tendency to mingle and confuse these two kinds of ideas led in this century to the 'value-free' position. Unfortunately, this was a false solution to the problem of fact and value, but it was one that came to be widely professed by serious thinkers on social and political questions. As a result, the values that distinguish liberalism from other social-political doctrines received little consideration, a circumstance which facilitated liberals' adoption of simplistic welfare statist notions after World War II.

The value-free position meant that in order to avoid the confusion of fact and value, as in wishful thinking, one would simply avoid any serious consideration of value questions as such, either in theoretical or practical contexts. It was widely assumed that value propositions, which express preferences, could not be rationally justified or refuted, as indeed they presumably cannot be when they are stated as universally binding rules. Thus one could consider the values and preferences of persons and groups only as factual matters; for example, their distributions in populations, their attitudinal and behavioural correlates, and so on. However, this disregarded the problem that values are an essential part of all policy statements and recommendations, and that any serious discussion of social and political matters is trivial or meaningless unless it assumes certain values.

It should be clear in retrospect that the intellectual dominance of this position during the middle fifty years of this century would have been impossible had serious value conflicts and dilemmas actually been seen to exist at the time. But for reasons already explained in chapter 1, these fifty years witnessed a coming together of ideological and policy positions. There were, of course, serious ongoing arguments between moderates and social radicals over such ideal conditions as 'democracy', 'socialism', 'capitalism' and 'communism'. However, during most of the period, from about 1920 to at least 1960, these differences were almost always seen as different routes to some vaguely 'liberal', generally 'democratic' society. Only the German Nazis and, to a lesser degree, the Italian Fascists openly resisted this vague, ultimately 'liberal democratic' standard.

It was not until the 1960s that many students of social and political matters, particularly among the young, insisted on bringing value considerations back into learned debate, and from there into public discussion. This change apparently arose from the discovery of growing discord between developed and developing societies and between insiders and outsiders in developed societies themselves. Unfortunately, however, this reaction amounted to little more than a simple repudiation of the value-free position. It innocently called for a return to the intermingling of fact and value considerations that was characteristic of pre-scientific philosophy. Thus it offered no immediate help in the confusions of liberal thought because clarification, correction and amendment required sophisticated, separate analyses of liberalism's valuational preferences and factual assumptions and of their relations with each other.

Like every position on public (or private) questions, liberalism contains value preferences, which establish goals, and it contains factual or instrumental assumptions about the courses of action that will best achieve these goals. Just like any other factual or instrumental assumptions, those belonging to liberalism are subject to validation or invalidation by experience. However, as a consequence of this century's general neglect of values as such, the distinction between liberalism's ultimate values and its instrumental assumptions has been lost. That is, the loose way in which liberal values are customarily formulated tends to make them subsume instrumental assumptions and hence to withdraw the latter from empirical test. This creates the extremely widespread tendency to treat key instrumental assumptions as ultimate values, thereby depriving liberalism of a plausible, analytically distinct and empirically testable instrumental doctrine

III

What are liberalism's basic value preferences? As developed originally by fairly well-situated 'bourgeois' strata between the seventeenth and nineteenth centuries, particularly in English-speaking countries and in parts of Northern Europe, liberalism emphasized freedom from arbitrary political and legal restraints and from interferences in legitimately private activites. Combining a belief in religious tolerance, a belief in freedom of speech for those who discuss issues responsibly, and a belief in the social utility and inherent fairness of freedom for economic entrepreneurs, it did not originally have any clear egalitarian bias.

During the nineteenth century, the Western countries, in which this doctrine was widely accepted, achieved political and economic domination over the world. Consequently, they all experienced a great increase in well-being, leisure and self-confidence within large categories of their populations. With this, many liberals found that political order and social peace in their countries was compatible with, and even facilitated by, wider and wider extensions of the suffrage. They discovered, in other words, that steadily increasing national power and prosperity and the multiplication of attractive and reasonably influential job opportunities permitted the formal democratization of their governments without opening the way to the likely participation of any great number of illiberal and highly discontented persons. Thus the English-speaking countries, the Low Countries and the Scandinavian countries in particular enjoyed obvious success in democratizing government and in extending internal liberal practices. Most other West European countries moved in similar directions, although elite disunity made their success less complete.

In this way, the attainment of stable liberal democracies gradually came to be seen as a plausible, even a natural progression, and liberals became increasingly committed to egalitarian values in terms of individual rights, including the right of suffrage. During the present century, this process led to the assumption that all the principal features of modern liberal democracies are equally components of liberalism's ultimate values. These features include (1) constitutional government, as distinguished from powerful monarchies and from military and other dictatorships that occur sporadically in unstable political systems; (2) political, administrative and judicial practices that strongly respect personal dignity by requiring that governments follow pre-established laws, that they put themselves at a substantial disadvantage in proving persons to be wrong-doers, and that they refrain from governing at all in certain more or less understood matters, such as religion and other forms of belief; and (3) democracy, in the sense at least of universal suffrage exercised in real contests that determine the leading governmental personnel.

Thus a liberal today is also normally a democrat, and the general pattern of government in the liberal societies of the West is called 'liberal democratic' to distinguish it from the professed 'people's democracy' of communist countries. However, while this evolution of liberalism into liberal democracy was natural enough in the historical economic and political contexts of the Western liberal countries, in most other countries the twin commitments to liberalism and democracy are often seriously in conflict. This is because opening effective political participation to all organized factions before a consensual unified elite, or at least an imperfectly unified elite, has been formed inevitably leads to political claims that are unacceptable to many entrenched interests in a society. Such interests are commonly numerous enough and well enough placed to carry out *coups d'état* that sweep away the threats to their way of life and privileges that come from the operation of democratic suffrage. Where entrenched interests do not manage to do this, moreover, revolutionary efforts to suppress them produce situations in which new elites find it necessary to firm up their rule by what in effect are curtailments of democratic liberties.

In most non-Western societies the prior construction of a consensual unified or imperfectly unified elite that is capable of managing democratic conflicts of interests has not occurred. Consequently, attempts to achieve liberal democracy merely by instituting democratic suffrage and holding elections are normally unsuccessful. This is amply illustrated by the repeated military *coups* that have terminated newly established democratic regimes in Latin America during the last century and a half. Since the abatement of colonial rule in the Middle East, South Asia and Africa, the general pattern of events in these areas has been the same.

Thus the linking of egalitarian goals such as democracy with liberal goals such as personal freedom and orderly government has involved considerable confusion, and by diverting attention from the requisite elite structures it has been generally harmful to the liberal cause. A more sophisticated understanding would see nearly all the features of modern liberal democracies as *instrumental* liberal values which under certain conditions may provide or promote *ultimate* liberal values. For example, while it seems clear that constitutional government and at least some version of governmental practice that respects personal dignity are empirically necessary to a liberal regime, democracy in the sense of an extended or universal suffrage is not strictly necessary, and in some circumstances it may even be inimical to such a regime.

To suppose that a liberal should ultimately prefer democratic government for its own sake is, in fact, a somewhat naive and provincial position. It is a position that is speciously plausible mainly to fairly well-off persons who happen to live under stable liberal regimes and whose favoured social circumstances enable them to derive direct personal satisfactions from democratic participation in their own government. But it has little plausibility for those who live under illiberal regimes or for less well-off and less self-confident persons in liberal states. In general, such persons have no interest in part-time, diligent excursions into the kind of limited negotiational politics that may offer considerable satisfaction to educated and relatively privileged citizens in liberal societies. Similarly, in contemplating liberal safeguards against violations of personal dignity, less well-off and less self-confident persons often conclude that these do less to protect their own dignities, which they may feel they have little of anyway, than they do to prevent effective control of the interests whom they fear or for whom they have no serious sympathy.

In order for liberal doctrine to obtain the allegiance of larger circles than the always limited number of well-off amateur politicians who like democratic politics for the fun it affords them, it is necessary to find in liberalism an ultimate value that can be more widely shared. At the same time, this value must be distinguished carefully from the instrumental values that may or may not contribute empirically to its realization.

We propose that the ultimate value preference of liberalism is for living in a society of 'free men'. That is, liberals ultimately prefer a society in which people deal with each other as equals and in which no one claims for himself, nor expects to accord to others, systematically greater deference or higher privilege. The expression 'free men' is used because of the historical contexts which it calls to mind, and it is not intended to exclude 'free women'. These historical contexts were those envisaged by liberals as ideal: the Rome of Horatio Cocles, the Switzerland of William Tell, the Holland of William the Silent, the America of George Washington. However, to invoke these contexts is to make it clear that it is only an active and somewhat individualistic freedom that makes equality valuable to liberals. They care nothing for, and even abhor, the kind of equality that might prevail in a community of unassertive persons who are wholly submissive to custom or to prevailing opinion.

Liberals view a social milieu in which persons are free and equal in active roles as an ultimate good. They believe that institutionalized politics and governmental practices which prevent violations of personal dignity contribute instrumentally toward achieving this milieu. Conversely, they believe that unstable politics involving *coups* and court intrigues, as well as governmental practices that readily degrade people, contribute instrumentally toward preventing or destroying such a milieu. As to democracy, or universal suffrage, its effectiveness as an instrumental device for achieving the desired milieu varies with circumstances.

This distinction between liberalism's ultimate and instrumental values implies that liberal attitudes normally require a substantial degree of good fortune, self-confidence and optimism about the future among those who hold them. This is because the opportunity to interact with other persons freely and equally is of little value to those who do not possess the kinds of occupational and social roles and the temperaments which facilitate such interaction. Without prior substantial changes in their situations, therefore, persons whose roles are seriously degrading, punishing, frightful or merely boring cannot be influenced toward, or converted to, liberalism. In other words, liberal attitudes can never be contagious except among people who are already disposed by a certain kind of good fortune to accept them.

In any complex, bureaucratized society, there is always a shortage of the kinds of roles which enable people to interact freely, vigorously and equally with each other. This means that in order to establish or preserve a liberal society, liberals may occasionally be morally obligated to 'give to him that hath' and 'from him that hath not take away even that which he hath'. For example, any commitment to 'social justice' that involves as a matter of *overriding principle* concessions to, or privileges for, persons and groups as recompense for their past misfortunes is strictly incompatible with a sophisticated allegiance to liberal values. When granted on a principled and wide basis, such special concessions and privileges threaten to undermine the advantaged positions of those who are already liberal. In doing this, they help to destroy liberal attitudes where they exist without providing any certainty that those being helped will themselves adopt such attitudes. No informed liberal could favour such schemes on a principled basis.

IV

Clarifying liberalism's ultimate and instrumental values in this way places the relationship of liberalism to democracy and other egalitarian measures on an entirely different footing from that which has been presumed in most recent political thought. If liberals ultimately prefer to associate with active free persons on a basis of equality, then obviously a society of 'free men' that is governed democratically and that is otherwise egalitarian is the liberal *ideal*. Liberals would greatly prefer this to an oligarchical society, for instance, in which only a small number of privileged people interact on a free and equal basis. Yet, the historical contingencies that have produced societies that are both liberal and somewhat egalitarian have been rare. They have mostly occurred in the Western countries that were advantaged over the rest of the world by their early technological progress. Indeed, any liberal who is reasonably familiar with history would not believe that this ideal is attainable in most circumstances. A society that is considerably more stratified but which nevertheless has an upper layer of free and equal persons (by no means a common historical circumstance) is the most that a liberal can normally hope to attain or preserve.

To achieve even this limited goal requires either highly propitious circumstances or shrewd and devious political engineering. In societies in which liberal practices do not exist, only those people who have accidentally escaped abuses by entrenched authority and privilege, or who have the character to resist the effect of such abuses on their own feelings, can possibly be liberals. For the most part in such societies, those who are well-off seek to retain a more or less assured power to hurt others, while those who are not well-off normally use every means to improve their situations and to take revenge against their real or imagined enemies. Even in established liberal democracies, as we have said, many less self-confident people do not value the relatively pugnacious give and take that is possible between free, equal and active individuals, while many openly discontented people readily strive for the systematic humiliation and degradation of those whom they hold responsible for their discontents.

These are reasons why liberal regimes have never been brought about or maintained merely by appealing directly to 'the people' to establish or adhere to liberal democratic values and procedures. Yet the naive notion that people normally *want* liberal democracy has been disastrously prevalent in twentieth-century liberal thought. This has been because the privileged and self-confident strata who have participated with satisfaction in the liberal politics of Western countries have conveniently, but erroneously, supposed that other people would also like to 'govern themselves' in this fashion. It has also been because these countries have been politically and economically dominant over most of the world during this century. As we said earlier, the largess garnered from this domination made it possible to democratize without mobilizing large, seriously discontented and openly illiberal population categories. The speciousness of generalizing from these propitious, very likely non-recurring, circumstances without analysing them causally has been amply shown by the persistent failure of stable liberal democracies to become established elsewhere in the twentieth century world.

Thus the relation of democracy and other forms of egalitarianism to liberalism is much more subtle than recent thinking has assumed. The liberal's preference is to interact somewhat individualistically with persons whom he can treat as equals and who will treat him as an equal. From his standpoint, therefore, the more socially or geographically extended an actual society of equal free persons is, the better it will satisfy him. If he were a magician he would make all persons and all nations able to live together in active and self-assertive equality. But there are no magicians in social and political matters, and there is no simple, straightforward way to create or extend a society of free and equal persons by political or legal means. It is obvious that, as socialists argue, one cannot make unequal persons equal merely by declaring them equally qualified to vote and to participate in formal politics, as in democracy. It is also obvious that one cannot make unequal persons equal merely by enforcing a variety of rules, principles and standards designed to prevent people from taking advantage of their inequality, as in socialism.

This is because the working of any complex social structure constantly puts persons in positions where they have leverage over others. Such position-holders normally take advantage of their leverage to obtain further advantages for themselves, their families and their friends. The only way this can be minimized is by a social structure that offers no serious advantages to anyone. But as we argued in chapter 2, apart from impoverished tribal situations, such egalitarian circumstances occur only, and then only temporarily, where a society consisting almost entirely of self-supporting farming and artisan families without a leisured aristocracy has come into existence in a thinly settled and resource-rich area.

While such a situation lasts, there is little opportunity for anyone to accumulate leverage or advantages over fellow settlers because there are no organizational niches to operate from. Consequently, at least male family heads are substantially equal in their rather limited dealings with each other. All such naturally egalitarian situations end, however, as soon as normal population growth requires more complex production and distribution arrangements. These are necessarily more extended bureaucratically and financially, and they contain positions from which persons can systematically control the range of choices open to others. Alternatively, a naturally egalitarian situation ends as soon as more organized and aggressive outsiders invade the area and impose some of their number as a privileged aristocracy.

Contemplating the less organized and less widespread commerce and bureaucracy of a hundred years ago in Western societies, socialists thought that they could impose limits on self-aggrandizement by abolishing private property in the means of production. That this would have been an effective measure in the nineteenth century societies for which it was originally proposed is highly doubtful, however, because all of them contained substantial bureaucratic organizations that could not have been dispensed with. Certainly making this measure effective in today's developed societies would require a drastic curtailment of the scale and extent of industrial, commercial and governmental organization. Not only is such organizational curtailment not contemplated by most contemporary socialists, but if it were tried its likely effect would be a disastrous reduction of productivity.

If the modern scale of organization is maintained, however, merely abolishing private property would be as purely formal and ineffective in assuring equality as is the effort to make people equal politically by declaring them eligible to vote. The socialist remedy for inequality is therefore as inherently ineffective as the democratic remedy. In practice, any socialist regime that retains the modern scale of organization sets up no basic barrier to individual aggrandizement. Such a regime can only attempt to maintain the *appearance* of equality by a variety of police measures, scapegoating, or occasional 'cultural revolutions' that penalize particular individuals who are noticed to have aggrandized themselves in objectionable ways.

But such abuses of successful persons, to which socialist regimes commonly resort, do not seriously curtail processes of social differentiation and stratification because these find a firm basis in bureaucracy and its accompanying specialization of function. Of course, if a socialist regime is also liberal and therefore committed to respecting personal dignity, it cannot seriously attempt equalization by police measures. If it is not liberal, it can make this attempt without any prospect of success.

These considerations raise a serious moral question which liberals have largely confused or overlooked during this century. Although his preference is for individualistic participation in a society of equal persons, is the liberal honestly an egalitarian? An egalitarian is presumably a person committed to the equalization of people as an intrinsic good. When this egalitarian preference is held unconditionally, it is likely to prove incompatible with the liberal preference for a society of free persons within which one can interact as an active equal.

It is simply a matter of fact that the liberal can sometimes find an approximation of his ideal that would probably be upset or destroyed in particular circumstances by egalitarian measures. For example, in eighteenth-century England a considerable number of well-off persons enjoyed an approximation of a liberal society in their own interactions, although most of the population was poor, uneducated, disfranchised, and liable to abusive treatment by the authorities if they expressed themselves or acted in ways that endangered the well-off. Yet it can hardly be supposed that in that time and place the liberal practices that existed would have survived at all if some force had decreed formal equality for all and then actually implemented this decree by the equivalent of today's affirmative action measures and confidence-building exercises in community action organizations for the deprived. Similarly, there can be little doubt that liberal practices in Western liberal democracies today would be destroyed if someone established a genuine world government with a full range of taxing and police powers and with arrangements designed to ensure that developing and communist countries exercised their proportionate shares of influence in policy-making.

In these sorts of situations, in other words, a liberal is prudently willing to accept his goal in the form of half a loaf if the alternative appears to be no bread. Therefore, he cannot honestly claim to be a committed egalitarian in the way in which some persons are, or believe themselves to be. He is willing to live in a society where liberal practice extends only to that part of the population to which he and his associates generally belong if further equalization can only be attained by upsetting the liberal character of the semi-society in which he participates. Likewise, he is willing to live in a group of liberal countries that enjoy considerable advantages in technology and in access to world resources over other countries if (1) international equalization is not attainable without drastically curtailing living standards in the advantaged countries such that their liberal practices would probably be destroyed, and if (2) because of the population ratios involved there is little prospect that international equalization would create liberal practices in the countries whose living standards would be minutely increased thereby.

The liberal is selfish, though he is not necessarily more selfish than the average person. This characterization is consistent, of course, with the ethics implicit in historical liberal doctrine that equated good with the rational self-interests of individual persons. In the affluent liberal societies of 1980, however, many persons who are otherwise inclined towards liberalism hope to find some more impersonal and universal basis for an intellectually respectable morality. While we do not share this axiological hope, it is worth pointing out to those who do that if full equality is as difficult or impossible to attain as we have contended, and if the establishment of liberal democracies was as historically unlikely and accidental as seems to have been the case, then a less individualistically based morality than liberalism would counsel to the liberal no serious modification of the selfishness imputed to him here. That is, any morality must come to terms with the more or less ineluctable aspects of social structure and behaviour to which we have pointed. When it does so, we do not expect that the conclusions would be radically different from those arrived at through a liberal calculus.

V

The liberal is necessarily an elitist, however this may clash with what he would prefer as an ideal if ideals could be made real. He has had, or expects to have, enough good fortune to make him want and value the equal interaction of free and actively individualistic persons. He is more self-confident, more self-reliant, and less fearful of powerful persons and interests than is the average person either historically or today. If he had no opportunity to sample liberal practices, or if he were less certain that he could hold his own when interacting freely with assertive persons, he would be more inclined, as most people are, to aims other than liberal ones.

The failure of liberals to recognize the elitist nature of their circumstances and goals, and their tendency to endorse egalitarian principles as if they were fully committed to them, have crippled the liberal movement during this century. These errors have made the movement unaware of its own instrumental needs, and they have incurred for it the enmity and contempt of less fortunate persons who, alienated by the obviously privileged situations of most liberals, see the latters' egalitarianism as a fraudulent pretence.

The liberal is not, however, commited to inequality. He is not among those who prefer a society of unequal and unfree persons in principle. He does not seek social advantages for himself as an ultimate goal. Rather, he accepts advantages when they afford him free and equal interaction with other persons and when there are no practical possibilities for widening the circle of liberal persons.

In his politics, the liberal is also an elitist as regards the desirability and feasibility of democratic practices. Here too, the failure to distinguish values or preferences from instrumental considerations has caused liberals to lose all understanding of the real relations of democracy to their aims during this century. By treating democratic government as an indistinguishable part of a cluster of goals, liberals have committed the otherwise hardly conceivable error of thinking that formal equality in political statuses, democracy, is a reliable means for promoting liberal practices. Considered on its own merits, this proposition that universal suffrage, frequent voting and other democratic measures reliably, that is, regardless of circumstances, promote the interaction of free and actively equal persons is patently incredible to persons with much political experience or knowledge.

It is more nearly the other way around. Especially among elites, fairly widespread liberal practice, manifested, for example, in no desire to use political means to accomplish drastic social changes, is essential to the year-in, year-out acceptance by different factions of a competition for votes that determines who shall hold office and who shall define policy. As we have stressed, a 'live and let live' attitude among powerful persons and groups, which means a tacit agreement not to exacerbate conflicts and to respect each other's vital interests, is the *sine qua non* for any practical and durable degree of democratic politics.

By contrast, in a society whose elites and other dominant elements are not liberal, those actually in political office at any given moment must fall into one of two categories. Normally, such office-holders represent advantaged strata that do not feel themselves to be secure against future contingencies. Such a political class will necessarily use political power, if they can, to further entrench themselves and those they represent by reducing the freedom of less fortunate strata to upset the regime in the future. Certainly they will not be restrained by notions of political freedom in taking such action. Instead, they will tolerate democratic practices only when it is convenient to themselves, and ordinarily this will not be for very long.

The other, less likely, category of political office-holders in a society where liberal practices are not firmly established is those who have been victorious in a recent revolutionary upheaval. Normally these persons hold egalitarian convictions. But they are well aware, as modern liberals are not, that an ordinary political class must act in the way just described. Consequently, while the egalitarians may well regard democratic self-government by 'the people' as appropriate to their convictions, they have no intention of letting the opportunity to reform society in an egalitarian direction slip through their hands. Certainly they will not take the chance of setting up an electoral competition that might be won by persons who do not share their principles. Instead, they will feel obligated to keep the electoral process effectively controlled in order to produce the results they approve of so long as they are able to do so. In short, they will not introduce the kind of democratic practices that would be of interest to liberals.

VI

Has the liberal's erroneous conception of himself and of the distinction between his ultimate and instrumental values prevailed too long to be reparable? Possibly it has. As the example of

Colonel House illustrates, many public leaders leaned toward this erroneous conception as early as World War I. Since at least World War II, almost everyone who might be considered a liberal has mistakenly characterized the ultimate liberal goal in egalitarian terms. The unanimity and fervour with which persons who think of themselves as liberals have until recently urged extensive democratizations of non-liberal developing societies indicate a near total confusion of cause and effect in their political analyses.

This confusion has greatly weakened the self-recognition of liberals to the point where it is uncertain whether liberal-minded elite and sub-elite persons are any longer capable of identifying and taking the kinds of initiatives that might deal constructively with the world's problems. For example, liberals fail to comprehend that in their own societies the spread of democratic suffrage in ways that did not fundamentally undermine liberal practice depended on the prior existence of consensual unified elites and probably also on substantial world economic domination. Thus, they do not comprehend that the absence of these conditions in most developing societies may necessitate less than democratic means of governing them. Until in some fashion elites in a developing country are consensually unified, attempts at democratic government are bound to fail.

Chapter 4
Elitism as obligation

In its restated form, the elitist paradigm has much factual significance, as well as considerable explicative and predictive force. It also has important normative and policy significance for the judgments and actions of relatively wide circles of persons, especially in developed societies. This does not involve prescribing new values. Rather, by clearly characterizing certain circumstances of political life that have been only vaguely appreciated, if at all, in recent Western culture, the elitist paradigm makes the established values of Western liberal thought point to several obligations that have not been apparent in the past.

I

Elite persons always have more power, and they usually have more wealth, status and privilege than others have. Because of this, the existence of elites is fundamentally incompatible with any full measure of freedom and equality in a society. This is why elitism, in the sense of an acceptance of elites, is usually correctly regarded as inimical to radical libertarian and egalitarian preferences. The basic normative implication of elitism is that in all developing and developed societies judgments about the possible or desirable extent of freedom and equality must be accommodated to the existence of elites.

To be sure, the elitist paradigm allows for more or less unlimited degrees of freedom and equality in undeveloped (Level 1) societies where there is little or no complex organization. Although such societies usually contain severely repressive and exploitative ruling classes, these are not an inescapable feature of undeveloped societies. Where especially defensible geography allows a population to guard its territory while engaging in subsistence agriculture, ruling classes can sometimes be avoided or driven off. When this happens, the heads of self-supporting families, and perhaps other family members, may enjoy substantial freedom and equality.

By contrast, in all even minimally urbanized societies, that is, in all developing (Levels 2 and 3) and in all developed (Level 4) societies, there is no alternative to rule by persons who are strategically placed in bureaucratic structures. These persons are best viewed as forming elites, rather than ruling classes, because their rulership derives from strategic organizational positions instead of memberships in specific families. This distinction in no way denies the advantaged positions of certain families over others in such societies, however. Elites, their relatives and their hangers-on to a large extent perpetuate themselves as advantaged people from generation to generation except as military conquerors or revolutionaries occasionally overthrow them, only to impose new elites in their place. So long as a society contains any seriously bureaucratic organizations there can never be more than a momentary absence of elites and their families.

While most persons would probably agree that this is a reasonably accurate depiction of the historical state of affairs, many are reluctant to conclude that it comprises a permanent limitation on possible degrees of freedom and equality. Instead, there is a widespread desire, especially in affluent Western societies, to believe that some great change away from the elitist element of complex, bureaucratically organized societies is possible if the proper political and social magic for bringing it about can be devised. The elitist paradigm denies this possibility, not only by emphasizing that such a change has never happened in the past, but also by specifying why it can never happen.

Every person has some inclination to advance himself, his close associates, and the collective interests with which he identifies, if there are opportunities to do so. In those undeveloped societies in which an hereditary ruling class has not established itself, there is little scope for such self-regarding action. This is because there is little need for the kinds of bureaucratic organizations that create serious personal power. If, in addition, social mores happen to oppose self-assertion, there is simply no context in which self-regarding actions of a sustained and cumulative kind can occur. In such cases, indeed, it sometimes proves difficult to prevail upon persons to perform public functions that elsewhere would be the subject of competition.

In any society that is even slightly more urbanized and developing, at least some bureaucratic organization of defence and police forces, of public works, transport and other activities is unavoidable. For example, even the crews of simple, wind-powered ships have always had to be hierarchically organized. If a society is more than barely developing, there will of course be many other forms of bureaucratic organization necessary to adapt and co-ordinate productive and distributive activities according to some prevailing definition of social needs. In such societies, therefore, certain people find themselves in strategic bureaucratic positions even if they do not seek them out. Most others do not.

A person in a strategic bureaucratic position normally discovers that its possibilities for influencing what happens in the world easily justify the time and attention that are required to learn how to perform its essentially political tasks and functions skilfully. By contrast, a person who is not in such a position ordinarily does not have sufficient incentives to cultivate political skills, even though community norms may stress general political participation. Consequently, the person not strategically placed seldom becomes a serious rival to the strategically placed, and therefore politically experienced, person. Even assuming the most egalitarian socialization and education systems, those who already possess some of the power of strategic bureaucratic positions find this power worth conserving, while those who do not possess it seldom find that developing the skills that might rectify their situation is worth the effort. This is a principal reason why elites always tend to perpetuate themselves, passing some of their advantages on to relatives, friends and allies.

Although social norms aimed at preventing this situation have occasionally been imposed in societies (for example, under communist regimes), these norms are never enforced to the extent necessary for success. This is because if they were strictly enforced the result would be a loss of interest in elite functions by those currently performing them, and consequently the careless and casual performance of bureaucratic functions by most other persons. This would quickly produce a serious weakening of economic and national defence organizations, to name but two areas of permanent concern to all societies. Similarly, reforms aimed at fostering the rapid turnover of influential position-holders through annual elections, recall ballots, early retirements and the like make it worth no one's while to learn to act skilfully and effectively in authoritative bureaucratic or political positions.

To summarize, where any serious division of labour prevails, only some persons can occupy strategically influential bureaucratic positions. These persons have the incentive to develop the kinds of political skills that are necessary to secure and hold such positions, and most other persons have little incentive to do so. This means that in societies of any complexity there is simply no way to prevent elitism. Therefore, all normative commitments to goal values such as freedom and equality must be tempered by this ineluctable aspect of complex social organization.

II

Preferences for the presence or absence of elites in developing and developed societies are, thus, pointless. Instead, the morally significant differences between these societies seem to relate to the internal cohesion of elites, the basis of this cohesion, and its social and political consequences. Relevant normative judgments pertain, in other words, to preferences for some kinds of elites over others, and to the wisdom of trying to modify or transform particular elites.

A few societies have consensual unified elites, the members of which tend to trust each other not to play the political game with too much risk to other elite participants. Consensual unified elites operate stable 'republican' regimes in which power is transmitted between elite factions and persons without *coups d'état* or other grossly irregular actions. Examples are the Venetian elite from far back in the Middle Ages until the end of the eighteenth century, the British elite after 1689, the Swedish elite after 1809, and the American elite after the Independence War.

A basic consensus about the desirability of existing institutions and procedures enables members of these elites to take opposing public positions on policy questions without unduly threatening each other. This involves co-operating tacitly to keep the public's consciousness of really divisive issues to minimal proportions. By limiting the expression of divisive issues, a consensual unified elite is able to give a large part of the public, rather than merely one section of it, some sense that government is responsive to popular wishes. Consequently, this is the only kind of elite that can allow fairly wide and reliable political freedoms. From the standpoint of liberal values, therefore, a consensual unified elite would seem to be the preferred alternative among those available.

Next most preferable by the same standard would be an imperfectly unified elite. This contains a sizeable, conservative portion of national leaders who have the same kind of internal cohesion as that which binds a consensual unified elite. However, a less powerful portion of leaders, who usually profess highly egalitarian values and policies and who therefore are generally excluded by the others from real power, are not similarly able to assure other elite persons that they play the political game without seriously threatening these other persons' statuses.

This peculiar kind of elite prevailed in Belgium throughout its modern history at least until 1960. It could be found in pre-World War II Norway and Denmark. It has clearly been in evidence in France, Italy and Japan during much of the post-war period. Imperfectly unified elites are moderately compatible with liberal values because they operate fairly stable representative governments in societies that have reached the development level at which a clear majority of non-elites reliably supports the conservative portion of the elite at elections.

The two other possible kinds of elites in developing and developed societies are strictly incompatible with liberal values. In the most common kind, the disunified elite, the historical events that seriously unify elite persons and enable them to trust each other have not occurred. Consequently, the initiatives for all important political actions grow out of deep elite rivalries, and there is no sense that government policy represents trends in popular preferences. Moreover, elite distrust is so sharp that respect for established institutions does not restrain elite factions from seeking their own advantage at any cost. Constitutions are therefore meaningless, and open seizures of power through raw force are frequent or are widely believed to be real possibilities. Although temporary lulls in elite rivalries allow attempts at representative government, serious political crises sooner or later abort these representative experiments and restore some form of dictatorship.

Finally, there is the ideological unified elite. This is created when the leadership of a fanatical mass movement manages to replace a pre-existing elite. Such movements are usually committed to strictly impossible political goals, but through totalitarian organizational devices their leaderships quickly become entrenched and self-perpetuating. Although two such elites, the Italian Fascists and the German Nazis, espoused a brand of populistic conservatism, most ideological unified elites have been committed, at least in theory, to a thorough-going egalitarianism, as in Russia, Eastern Europe and some Asian countries. In all these cases, an elite of strategically influential persons has preserved the usual perquisites and advantages of elite status. None has avoided heavy-handed repression of real or suspected dissidents, and each has been ruthless in stifling non-elite opinion and sacrificing some elite persons as scapegoats for inevitable policy failures. For these reasons, ideological unified elites are anathema from the standpoint of liberal values.

To summarize, the elitist paradigm presents a clear ordering of normal preferences for the person who holds liberal values such as political freedom, and practical degrees of democracy and of equality of opportunity. It clearly behoves a liberal person to support and perpetuate regimes operated by consensual unified elites under ordinary circumstances. Where such regimes do not exist and cannot be brought about, those operated by imperfectly unified elites should normally be preferred. On the other hand, a liberal would abhor regimes operated by ideological unified elites. Likewise, he has no preference for regimes operated by disunified elites except in so far as the only available alternatives might be regimes with ideological unified elites.

III

Among the political possibilities identified by the elitist paradigm, the normative superiority of regimes operated by consensual unified elites, and secondarily of those operated by imperfectly unified elites, is clear. But the paradigm provides no equally clear prescriptions about how to bring these elites and regimes into existence where they do not already exist. Indeed, it indicates that, except in cases of military conquest and the imposition of foreign rule, changing the form of disunified or ideological unified elites can only be accomplished by elite persons themselves.

This is because efforts by non-elites to force particular elite factions in one or another direction will, if effective, merely make already insecure elite persons even less secure. And this can only make trusting, co-operative elites, and stable, reasonably representative governments less, not more, likely. Efforts by foreign elites to change the form of a particular country's elite through international pressures will normally have the same result. Even military conquest by outside forces is most likely to perpetuate or to produce one of the two unacceptable forms of elites.

This means that the prescriptions to be drawn from the paradigm often take the form of discouraging reckless, short-sighted measures which seek to bring about changes that are, in fact, impossible. In dealing with totalitarian regimes operated by ideological unified elites, for example, nothing is to be gained by merely disregarding the political limits involved. Individual dissent will simply not be tolerated where elite unity depends on the enforced profession of a single ideology. Among other things, the existence of a totalitarian party penetrating all strata and organizations blocks the communication channels through which dissent could spread to the extent that it would become difficult to repress. In totalitarian regimes, the individual dissenter, his friends and associates can only expect severe penalization. Except as a means of avoiding serious individual moral compromise, therefore, dissent in such a regime is pointless.

It is similarly pointless for foreign elites to disregard these political limits unless they intend to displace the ideological unified elite in question by force. While casual expressions of sympathy for those who are oppressed by such an elite may be appropriate, any serious 'human rights' campaign to increase the tolerance of ideological unified elites for dissenters can only be expected to have negative results. Indeed, because they may encourage dissenters to overexpose themselves and to suffer severe punishments, such campaigns can be considered immoral.

This does not deny that circumstances might arise in which a totalitarian regime operated by an ideological unified elite would be vulnerable to internal opposition movements. However, historical experience shows that such circumstances are extremely unlikely to occur, at least during the first or second generation of totalitarian rule. Ordinarily, efforts to encourage organized opposition in totalitarian regimes are bound to fail, and ordinarily the consequences for those drawn into such opposition movements are highly unfortunate.

Internal or foreign sponsored opposition to a dictatorial regime operated by one faction in a disunified elite is just as pointless if its purpose is not merely to substitute one dominant clique for another. Dictatorships, military juntas and the like are usually not as firmly entrenched as totalitarian regimes. If the armed forces are at all disaffected, such dictatorships and juntas may be over-thrown rather easily. The difficulty is, however, that as long as the elite remains disunified, there can be nothing that is both preferable (as a general type of regime) and stable to put in place of the overthrown regime. Thus the heroics of rebellion, even when apparently successful, can ordinarily produce no new type of regime. At most, a successful rebellion affords purely tempor-ary relief from persecution to certain factions and movements. But only another dictatorship can offer any degree of stability, and no one who has participated in the overthrow of one dicta-torship can count on the next one protecting his specific interests, much less political freedom generally.

Frequently, the overthrow of a dictatorship is followed by the attempt to establish processes of representative government. But unless the elite in question becomes consensually unified at the same time, this can mean no serious or permanent elimination of dictatorial rule. If the elite remains disunified, then the mere practice of representative politics will constantly produce what various elite factions perceive as threats to their security and interests. This happens because no elite faction trusts other fac-tions to co-operate in containing the potentially explosive conflicts that regularly occur in any society. On the contrary, each suspects the others of fuelling and using these conflicts in order to gain the upper hand.

In this way, representative politics under disunified elites quickly become a series of crises that is usually terminated at some fairly early point by the imposition of a new dictatorship. Periods of representative government under disunified elites are in effect temporary interludes between dictatorial regimes – even if, some-times, as with the French Third Republic, these may be acciden-tally long-lasting. That such interludes are themselves often brought about primarily through politics within the military, and not through any serious shifts in public opinion, merely reinforces this observation.

For meaningful change towards politics that are congenial to liberal values, then, a full or partial consensual unification of elites is essential. But neither liberally motivated action by non-elites nor by foreign elites seems ordinarily capable of accomplishing this because of the politically delicate manoeuvres that are required.

The consensual unification of a disunified elite requires that elite persons lessen their allegiance to non-elite followings at the same time that they tighten their relationships with previously hostile elite factions. Under highly unusual circumstances in societies at a low level of development (Level 2), this has occasionally been accomplished, as in England in 1688–9, Sweden in 1809 and Mexico in 1933. But because of the greater range and strength of non-elite interests that assert themselves once societies reach a higher development level (Level 3), elites in more industrialized societies may have insufficient freedom to carry out such deliberate unifications. To judge by historical precedent, this would mean that for the large number of countries with disunified elites in the middle ranges of development today there is little or no chance of a consensual unification of their elites, and thus little or no chance of achieving stable, representative governments.

However, when a society approaches the highest level of development (Level 4), an imperfectly unified elite may manage to form, as for instance in France, Italy and Japan after World War II. If this happens, and if economic and other conditions are such that they contribute to reducing elite and non-elite tensions, then a gradual reconciliation of the more egalitarian elite faction with the electorally dominant conservative one may produce a consensual unified elite. In this situation, as in others, however, efforts by foreign elites to encourage the process are unlikely to be successful.

To summarize, the elitist paradigm holds that elites themselves are the pivotal actors if there is to be any basic change in the nature of a society's politics. Even though they may intend to act wholly in service to liberal values, non-elite persons, and leaders of other societies, can usually do little or nothing to promote the consensual unification of a disunified elite. Worse, the historical and contemporary evidence is overwhelming that disunified elites are rarely able or inclined to undertake deliberate unifications themselves.

Possibly it has been the past failure of disunified elites to understand the elitist paradigm's specification of their pivotal roles that has made deliberate elite unifications such rare events. On this reading, the efforts of elites to represent conflicting non-elite interests, as intellectually dominant notions about democracy prescribe, have hindered moves to establish collective elite security. This seems especially true of the disunified and imperfectly unified elites caught up in the sharp conflict between propertied conservative and wage-earning egalitarian interests that has pervaded both elite and non-elite politics in virtually all industrial (Level 3) societies. In the eyes of the different factions in these elites, something like a betrayal of supporters seemed to be involved in seeking the approval and trust of elite persons belonging to opposing factions.

In the heat of this struggle, in other words, widespread acceptance of the democratic injunction that elites should represent their followers fully and openly has obscured, and made illicit, the concern of elites for their own safety. Yet the desire to achieve greater security through the establishment of mutual trust and cooperation is an essential elite motivation in the process of consensual unification. Perhaps wider knowledge of the elitist paradigm and its acceptance as a more realistic definition of political possibilities may help to overcome this difficulty. In other words, once it is generally recognized that representative politics cannot operate successfully without the mediation of an internally trusting and collectively secure elite, then currently disunified or imperfectly unified elites may become more capable of consensual unification than history has shown them to be.

IV

Although there are strong reasons for preferring consensual unified elites over all other possibilities, even this preference is in some way conditional. For long periods before the twentieth century, English, Swedish, American and other consensual unified elites maintained stable political regimes which, though organized according to the principles of representative government, nevertheless excluded large categories of their citizens, mostly poor people, from the suffrage. Some persons, most notably the American Negroes, were additionally deprived of personal liberty or placed in dramatically subordinate statuses. Although these regimes could not reasonably be called 'democratic', in the context of their time they were liberal and probably preferable to other regimes of the day from the standpoint of most of their inhabitants.

At the time of this writing, there are at least two regimes, in South Africa and Zimbabwe Rhodesia, which appear to be operated by consensual unified elites, but which keep large segments of their populations in degraded subordinate statuses without political rights and subject to drastic discrimination. Both these regimes pose a moral dilemma for the elites of countries with stable, broadly representative governments, as well as for all other persons who might accept the elitist paradigm.

In South Africa and Rhodesia, persons of European descent have long held privileged positions. They have been numerous enough to maintain powerful defence forces and to keep political regimes going largely by themselves. In consequence, the excluded black populations have developed deep resentments, and many blacks are irreconcilably opposed to continued rule by whites. Although the elites in these countries have seemed (at least until 1979) to be consensual unified, this has been of no value to the black populations. The point has apparently been long passed where these regimes' stability did not depend on a terrorization of their black populations. Whatever their members' personal preferences might be, South African and Rhodesian elites are in effect committed to this terrorization because their authority depends on military and police forces who see themselves as targets of black resentment and who, therefore, must react with brutality and without regard for individual justice when dealing with assertive blacks.

Although South African and Rhodesian whites have previously enjoyed the regularity and fairness of political and judicial procedures that are normally associated with consensual unified elites, in recent years they have more and more experienced the features of desperate garrison states. Increasingly, moreover, they are themselves victims of black terrorism. If, as now seems highly likely, the white elites in these countries are eventually toppled by black resistance, with or without the aid of communist powers, the new, black elites which replace them will almost certainly be either disunified or, possibly, ideologically unified. This is because the black population's leaders have had virtually no experience in the processes of representative politics and, therefore, promise to be badly divided along tribal and other lines unless they are unified by some ideological mass movement.

One effect of these new black elites' ascendance will be a turning of the tables involving considerable persecution of whites.

Assuming that the territorial integrity of South Africa or Zimbabwe Rhodesia remains intact, a second effect of new black elites or, less dramatically, of a sudden addition of numerous blacks to the pre-existing white elites, will be substantial regressions from these countries' high levels of socioeconomic development (which appears to be Level 4 for the white population in Rhodesia and Level 3 in South Africa). Because they have applications beyond southern Africa it is worth pausing to elaborate the reasons why such regressions are probable.

Elite statuses are functional arrangements of persons within bureaucratic structures. They are not merely rights to participate from time to time in legislative bodies, trade union councils, corporate boards of directors, or other formal decision-making organs. Rather, they involve doing things within ongoing bureaucratic organizations that validate the 'strategic' character of elite positions. This entails understanding the business of one's office and using that office so that greater or lesser portions of the adjacent bureaucracy do not become inoperative or operative for purposes other than those intended. In other words, what makes persons who hold strategically influential bureaucratic positions 'elite' is not mere incumbency but the *use* of their positions in strategically influential ways.

Unfortunately, the leaders of oppressed majority castes normally operate in the world of conspiracy and paramilitary action. They are necessarily preoccupied with expressing mass grievances in highly simplified ways and with exploiting these in order to provoke acts of defiance against established regimes. Consequently, they have few opportunities to learn the specific technical skills that are essential to keeping complex bureaucracies functioning. More important, only where their learning occurs within resistance movements that are internally based on transactional or representative politics, such as the Indian National Congress or the Tanganyika African National Union, do they acquire the kinds of political skills that the existence of elite consensus and unity presume. Yet, resistance movements like these are rare. Normally, the leaders of rebellious castes and oppressed groups fail to acquire such skills.

Applying these considerations to the South African and Rhodesian examples, there is as yet little evidence that the black leaders who in the future might seek to form, or else to join, consensual unified elites in these countries would bring with them political skills acquired through familiarity with the subtleties of representative politics. Nor is there much evidence that they would bring the kinds of vocational knowledge that their individual positions in highly complex, technically sophisticated bureaucratic organizations would require. Thus eventual black triumphs in South Africa and Zimbabwe Rhodesia would mean not only new persons in elite positions, but also qualitatively different elite statuses.

Quite apart from war damage, an exodus of capital, the disorganization of productive enterprise and other setbacks that may attend the ascendance of these black elites, this would be sufficient by itself to force a sharp reduction in level of development. While this would clearly affect whites severely, it would probably also drastically reduce overall productivity and the ability to purchase goods in international markets. The decline in living standards among whites and blacks could extend to outright famine. In fact, beginning in 1975 something similar to this transpired in Kampuchea where a two-caste ethnic situation no longer prevailed, but where a dogmatically egalitarian leadership without any substantial bureaucratic or political experience imposed itself as the new elite.

These considerations eliminate what on a simplistic basis might seem to be one normative implication of the elitist paradigm. This is that in countries such as South Africa and Zimbabwe Rhodesia liberal values counsel a sudden opening or reorganization of the elite to include a proper proportion of blacks so that 'reasonable' blacks and whites might cooperate in future development. Even assuming that 'reasonable' whites would consent to this, there are probably not enough black persons politically and otherwise skilled enough to take over the functions of the eliminated white leaders within a consensual unified elite. In short, a settlement of the racial conflicts in these countries, as they are now territorially constituted, without retroactive development and with the continuation of consensual unity among the elite is simply not available.

Unless some way of transcending existing political borders presents itself, therefore, Western countries committed to liberal values would do well to stay as aloof as possible from concrete proposals for solving these problems. If blacks eventually emerge from their lower-caste statuses in South Africa and Rhodesia, this will involve drastically unhappy events for the white minorities, and probably for the black majorities as well. It would be inex-

pedient for Western political leaders to bear responsibility for the
general scheme under which these events come about.

V

The unlikelihood of any liberal settlement to racial conflicts in
Southern Africa does not mean, however, that oppression of racial
or ethnic groups cannot be drastically curtailed or eliminated
under consensual unified elites. Such a process has clearly been
under way in the United States for several decades. It could occur
in countries such as Britain, the Netherlands and West Germany
which have added significantly disadvantaged racial and ethnic
groups to their populations since World War II.

The first and essential condition for a curtailment of ethnic
discrimination under a consensual unified elite is that the
aggrieved groups do not constitute, as they do in Southern Africa,
large proportions of the population in question. This is essential
because when such groups are clear minorities justice does not
demand that an overwhelming portion of the elite be eventually
drawn from them.

A second condition that is at least helpful is that racial and
ethnic minorities are dispersed geographically. Dispersion tends
to militate against a uniform system of oppression. In the United
States, for example, there has always been a great deal of geographic diversity in the nature and degree of racial and ethnic
oppression. One section of the country had a caste system which
involved official discrimination against the principal minority
group, the blacks. In the rest of the country, blacks were concentrated in urban neighbourhoods in conditions that made attainment of occupational and social equality unlikely. While racial
prejudice was widespread as an individual sentiment of whites,
only in the South was it part of any official, recognized doctrine.
Outside the South it had little or no sanction in law, and blacks
commonly voted and took part in political organization in minor
and restricted ways. Since blacks in the North were concentrated
in specific urban areas, and since their deprivations were at least
partly linked to the cultural background which they had brought
North with them, few whites outside the South had any acute
sense of discriminating against them. Following the ostensible

liberal norms of American political culture, moreover, elite persons ordinarily denied any intention of discrimination.

Once blacks in the South began to protest vigorously against the official system of discrimination, elite persons in the rest of the country widely condemned the Southern system and sought to end it. In these circumstances, legal and formal political discrimination against blacks in the South was wiped out in a very short time. In both North and South, blacks soon began appearing in official and responsible positions, although a full equalization of the aggregate statuses of blacks and whites has not occurred.

In the North in particular, relatively few blacks have managed to escape from the central city ghettos. This is less a manifestation of continuing racial discrimination, however, than of what we have called the 'outsider' problem in all developed (Level 4) societies. The causes of this problem are much broader than racial or ethnic discrimination, although this distinction hardly constitutes grounds for complacence about racial and ethnic inequalities in the United States or elsewhere. The point, in any case, is that, because of the special conditions of minority groups in the United States, the American political system has reacted to protests against discrimination and oppression in a fashion wholly different from that of the southern African regimes.

To recapitulate, although all three countries have had consensual unified elites and representative political systems, in South Africa and Zimbabwe Rhodesia any fair solution to racial oppression involves an almost total substitution of black for white elite persons. This has not been the case in the United States because blacks and other minorities do not comprise such large fractions of the total population. In Southern Africa the repression of blacks has necessarily been so systematic and official that members of the white elites have become committed to it. They are well aware that it cannot be abandoned without disastrous consequences for themselves and the white minority in general. By contrast, large portions of American elites and non-elites have not been consciously involved in maintaining a discriminatory system. In fact, political traditions have tended to influence many Americans against discrimination. This means that a large part of the American population has had no principled objection to a gradual rise in black statuses. For their part, American blacks could more easily accept gradual improvements because their numbers do not justify any large participation in elite circles and because there are grounds for viewing the existing white elites as at worst neutral and at best benevolent with respect to their aspirations.

The experience of the United States in alleviating racial and ethnic oppression implies, theoretically, a conceivable solution to the Southern African conflicts. Abstractly, at least, it implies that the South African and Rhodesian situations could be altered markedly if the political arenas involved were enlarged. That is, if racial oppression in those countries could be placed in a larger political jurisdiction, just as the American South has been part of a larger polity, then a promotion of black statuses and political participation, eventually producing self-governing elites of mixed racial composition, might be possible.

To the extent that this is theoretically possible, black political leaders in Africa have been right in seeking to reimpose British colonial rule as a means of bringing about a satisfactory settlement in Zimbabwe Rhodesia. However, these leaders have been unrealistic in supposing that Britain still has the economic strength and the domestic political stamina necessary for such a venture. Any similar effort to reimpose colonial rule on South Africa by Britain, the United States or any other power would, of course, be fantastic under present conditions. Certainly no Western liberal regime could today undertake the cost in lives and money that would be involved for the minimum period of years required to carry out real reform. Even if lives and money were bearable costs, moreover, the stern form of colonial rule that the intervening country would have to impose initially would be politically unsupportable at home.

Could an enlargement of the South African and Rhodesian political arenas be accomplished by the United Nations? Many Third World countries would probably be attracted to the idea that only through UN intervention could a southern African bloodbath, followed by serious retrogressive development from the moment black rule was imposed, be avoided. Nevertheless, in the current world situation the rivalry of the superpowers would probably prevent adoption of a workable system. It would seem to be impossible to establish a UN governing authority with sufficient discretion over a number of years to carry through the changes required.

There is another theoretical possibility for a smaller area like Rhodesia, however. A joint occupation by a number of neighbouring African states can be imagined, although the availability of sufficient military force is doubtful. This would have to be sponsored by the United States, Britain and the other Western countries in order to discourage reliance of the occupying countries on the Soviet Union for aid. How would this occupation differ from the triumph of native Rhodesian guerrilla forces over a white or mixed regime?

At least one of the neighbouring African states, Tanzania, seems to have a consensual unified elite. There are indications that this kind of elite may also be established in Zambia, Malawi and Kenya. These are countries that have enjoyed independence for some time. Their elites are used to independence and are no longer as actively resentful against continuing white influence and privilege as are the black populations in Rhodesia and South Africa. These neighbouring elites would almost certainly regard socioeconomic regression in Rhodesia as sufficiently harmful to general regional interests so that the price of retaining some whites in positions of limited authority for a generation or so might be worth paying. Indeed, the Kenyan elite has willingly paid this price throughout its economically successful two decades of sovereignty.

These suggestions are offered, however, to illustrate the meaning of the elitist paradigm, rather than as serious contributions to the diplomatic problem. In all cases the dimensions of manpower and geography are probably not right to permit interventions that would lead to benign solutions. For the diplomatic problem, as it affects outside Western powers, we can only repeat the admonition not to become excessively involved.

VI

Statements implying an ethical obligation to support a consensual unified elite in all normal circumstances presume that the breakup or serious reorganization of the territory over which such an elite presides are not in question. However, if persons holding liberal values felt excluded or disadvantaged by their ethnic statuses in such a territory, might they not legitimately prefer secession or a radical devolution of the territory's power structure? Under the elitist paradigm, what considerations should such persons weigh in deciding how to act in these circumstances?

After a long period in which Western nation-states were

enlarged and centralized, a number of movements with strong ethnic and geographic bases have suddenly emerged during the last fifteen years or so. As a consequence, the propriety of secession or some substantial devolution of power to regional authorities has unexpectedly come onto the political agenda. Although ethnically-based secessionist movements are fairly common in developing societies, the ones we have in mind have sprung up in developed societies that have long traditions of stable representative government under either consensual unified or imperfectly unified elites. The nature of the problem can best be characterized by sketching the particular circumstances of the most conspicuous cases.

Canada has long been a bilingual society. French-speakers are concentrated in the Province of Quebec, along with a minority of English-speakers. The English language has been predominant in the rest of the country, although there are a considerable number of people who might more conveniently speak French (or some other language). The *de facto* dominance of English did not give rise to serious political resentment until about 1960 when Quebec began to catch up with the rest of the country in urbanization and modernization. Suddenly, a Quebec secessionist movement arose that sought, among other things, to reserve influential positions within Quebec to French-speakers. Somewhat belatedly, the federal authorities in Ottawa tried to counter this movement by seeking to impose real bilingualism on what had been a largely English-speaking national civil service.

Since it seceded from the Netherlands in 1830, *Belgium* has been sharply divided into a Dutch linguistic culture in the north among Flemings, and a French linguistic culture in the south among Walloons. As in Canada, the problem was muted until after World War II by the fact that one linguistic group, the Flemings, was long less modernized and assertive. Most successful Flemings, in fact, spoke French and participated without difficulty in the business and politics of a predominantly French polity. Unlike the French in Canada, however, the Flemings comprise a distinct majority of the Belgian population. Once the tables were turned by modernization in the Flemish area, it clearly became the dominant part of the country politically.

As in Quebec, Flemish movements mounted sharp attacks on the privileged position of the rival culture, presumably with the idea of reserving influential positions in the Flemish area to the

Dutch-speaking. Comprising a minority that is no longer as economically advanced as the Flemings, the Walloons lack the political
power to resist a general shift of influence to the Flemings. Consequently, the use of French is now largely discontinued in the
Flemish area, and Walloon institutions have been forced to
migrate from it. Since the Walloons apparently have no desire to
join France, the main current problem in Belgium lies in the
awkward circumstance that its capital, Brussels, is a largely
French-speaking city located deep within Flanders.

Three similar cases of potentially secessionary nationalist movements are in the United Kingdom, a polity that until a moment
ago, so to speak, was generally regarded as thoroughly consolidated and stable.

A majority of the population in *Northern Ireland* is Protestant,
and a minority is Catholic. The area remained part of the United
Kingdom in 1921 when the rest of Ireland acquired independent
institutions. Then as now the British were unwilling to force the
northern Irish into a union with the Catholic south which many
of the northern Irish sharply opposed. The British parliament
delegated to Northern Ireland a wide area of self-government
through a local, democratically elected parliament and a cabinet
responsible to it. This arrangement polarized the two religious
culture blocks. Constituting a majority, the Protestants were
totally in control of government in the area, and the Catholics
were totally and permanently excluded from power. Beginning in
the late 1960s, this resulted in a sort of endemic civil war that
compelled the British to resume direct government of the area
and to use military forces in policing it. Terrorist activity has
become widespread. But the Irish government does not wish to
annex Northern Ireland in its present condition, and the British
government pays a considerable price in attempting to maintain
order. Some of the more extreme Protestants would probably
prefer independence because the British are unwilling to back up
Protestant interests systematically against the Catholics.

In early modern times the dominant classes of *Wales* became
assimilated to the English culture and language. A Welsh folk
culture and the distinct Welsh language continued in rural areas,
but for a very long time neither showed any signs of political self-
assertion. Meanwhile, migration and assimilation made most
of the population, especially in the cities, English-speaking.
Recently, however, a movement partly influenced by the Scots

nationalists and demanding substantial devolution of power to Welsh authorities has come into prominence. Having grown out of a movement that aimed simply at preserving Welsh culture, the Welsh nationalists are now committed to a revival of the language.

Although the culture of *Scotland* is in many ways distinct from English culture, there seems to have been no serious Scottish independence movement between the more or less voluntary merger of the two countries in 1707 and the 1960s. Over most of that period Scots who were more assertive and ambitious often migrated to England or to other parts of the British Empire. Their frequent successes in business and politics seem to indicate that they encountered no serious barriers to participation in the institutions and practices of British business or political power. On the average, those who remained in Scotland did not achieve English living standards, but in spite of this they were not heard from in any serious national sense until the 1960s. In Scotland there is no substantial remnant of speakers of a language other than English. Thus the common linguistic element that underlies most ethnic movements is absent in the Scottish case.

The Scottish movement's arguments have been relatively matter-of-fact in tone. There is no serious involvement with violence and terrorism. One is tempted to conclude that the basic circumstance behind this recent assertion of Scottish nationalism has been the disappearance of the British Empire. The English economy is no longer a sharply positive force with which to identify, and it is quite easy to argue that in some cases fiscal and economic measures suitable to English conditions have been unsuitable for Scotland. Thus the Scots Nationalists' case has been mainly an argument that in present conditions, and assuming possession of the bulk of British North Sea oil, an independent Scots economy could be more prosperous than the English or combined British economy is likely to be.

It is by no means certain that any of these movements will reach the point of actual secession, although serious devolution of governmental powers to distinct culture areas is already taking place in Belgium, and the Canadian provinces have always had wide power. The situation of Northern Ireland is peculiar since, as with the problems of South Africa and Zimbabwe Rhodesia, there may be no liberal solution available. British responsibility for the area represents a heavy drain on the British polity. On the other hand, British withdrawal, by forcing the intervention of Ireland to protect the Catholic minority, might upset the Irish elite's consensus and unity.

In the Belgian case, in spite of the prolonged bitterness of the quarrel, there is really nothing much more at stake. Completely separate Flemish and Walloon culture areas are now a foregone conclusion. The cultural status of French-speakers in Brussels and its suburbs remains a problem, however. Presumably, a formula defining the cultural rights of French-speakers who spill over from the capital into the surrounding Flemish area will eventually be agreed upon. The novelty of a country with a capital of one language and a population majority of another will probably exacerbate the tone of Belgian politics for a long time. Yet, there would appear to be little that can be done about this.

In the other three cases, Quebec, Wales and Scotland, choices as to how much ethnic separatism is worth and how to judge it against the preservation of larger and more efficient political areas are still open to elites and non-elites. It is not obvious that the breakup of Canada and Britain, which have consensual unified elites, would preclude the continuation of this kind of elite in the seceding areas. This being the case, there is little that the elitist paradigm can directly contribute to the ethical problems involved.

It is important to recognize that in all three situations we are presumably dealing with a political decision that will be determined by non-elite sentiments. If non-elites in Quebec, Wales and Scotland come to identify overwhelmingly with these areas because of a desire to protect themselves from outside competition for jobs, there will be little that elites can do to modify the result. On the other hand, if Canadian and British loyalties persist widely in the relevant areas that will also be decisive. It is difficult to see how elite operations can materially change the consequences of popular choice in these situations in any short period of time.

VII

If we now approach the subject of elitism as obligation more systematically, we must do so by observing first that every person, whether elite or non-elite, has his place 'in history'. That is, past events associate each person with some categories of persons more than with others. Inescapably, these associations incline persons toward certain political actions and away from others. Thus, the ordinary politics of rival interest groups goes on continuously under a consensual unified and imperfectly unified elite, it occurs fairly constantly under a disunified one, and it even occurs in limited ways under an ideological unified elite.

Where elites are consensually or imperfectly unified, interest group politics, together with varying degrees of coercion against discontented persons and groups, perform an essential function. This is the provision of as much peace as is possible in complex societies. Where elites are disunified, however, interest group politics are inevitably restrained, interrupted, and distorted by the various crises that the lack of proper elite mediation of issues produces. As a consequence, there is very little peace in such societies. Where elites are ideologically unified, much expression of interest group positions is distorted or totally silenced, just as the expression of more general discontents is largely prevented by constant coercion. In these societies the peace that exists is that of the graveyard.

Interest group politics goes on indefinitely, especially under consensual unified elites, and it never has a definite result. Certainly it never results in utopia – the just society. Instead, political outcomes are always advantaging some persons and groups while disadvantaging others. All that can be said is that while interest group politics are unavoidable in any complex society, the associations that give rise to them do not normally constitute a compulsion to engage in actions that people know to be futile or counter-productive.

The essential lesson of elitism is that many of the interest group actions that other paradigms recommend are either futile or counter-productive. For example, elitism portrays all utopias as strictly unattainable. It sees all possible political conditions as containing some injustices. Therefore, it implies that actions intended to bring about one or another utopian condition can do little more than satisfy desires for revenge and retaliation. By more clearly specifying this truth, elitism implies that such actions cannot be justified.

As we have stressed throughout this chapter, the principal ethical obligations of elitism are always related to a strong general preference for a consensual unified elite over other possibilities. This assumes, however, that the continuity of the society in question is not at issue and that inequalities within the society do not reach the point of gross discriminations according to race, ethnicity, or region. Even where such discriminations exist, there is still a strong preference for maintaining a consensual unified elite if one is in place, unless the elite is seriously caught up in the discriminatory practices and the group discriminated against is so large that no relief is possible without a disastrous substitution of politically untrained, inexperienced and unreconciled persons in elite positions. Where this situation is the case, as in Southern Africa, all that elitism counsels is to expand the area of effective political jurisdiction should there be any chance to do so.

In combination with modern technological productivity, the workings of a consensual unified elite promise to reduce, and perhaps eventually eliminate, other forms of discrimination, for example between social classes and between the sexes. Such discrimination was virtually universal a century ago, but developed Western societies with consensual unified elites have managed to truncate it sharply during the last hundred years. Class or sexual discrimination is, therefore, not a proper reason for undermining a consensual unified elite. Certainly elitism's denial of the possibility of utopias clearly bars any radical protest actions arising from this discrimination that would bring about a worse condition, namely the imposition of an ideological unified elite.

Except under the specific conditions of racial oppression referred to above, leaders and other persons who understand the elitist paradigm have an obligation to maintain an existing consensual unified elite. Undoubtedly, they are also obliged to protect and to further the interests with which they sympathize. But this must not be done at the cost of risking a disruption of elite unity and consensus, and it must never be done in pursuit of unattainable utopian goals.

Beyond this, leaders and others who understand the paradigm have an obligation to do what they can to bring about elite consensus and unity where it does not currently exist. In many instances, this means that there is an obligation to avoid the simplistic, misguided promotions of 'progress' that spring from other paradigms. In seeking to replace elite disunity with elite consensus and unity, for example, merely urging more democratic procedures and a wider tolerance of free expression is unlikely to be helpful. This is because in any society the opening up of political debate exacerbates political tensions. When this occurs extensively under disunified elites (as distinct from cosmetic changes designed to look well abroad), it simply brings closer the moment when the next *coup d'état* gives some elite factions greater security by suppressing their rivals.

No negotiated, deliberate unification of a disunified elite has ever occurred in a society that has progressed beyond a rather low level of development. However, this does not mean that such a unification could not be arranged if the prospect was sufficiently attractive to all or most factions in a disunified elite. In fact, in a world in which permanently rising living standards seem increasingly problematic for most societies, more and more elite and non-elite persons are likely to see such unification as clearly advantageous. In other words, with more sober assessments of future prospects, it will not be regarded as expedient merely to wait for the precarious, imperfect elite unifications that seem to occur once societies reach high development levels.

If the realization spreads that such gradual solutions to political hostilities are less and less certain, then it is possible that disunified elites who understand the processes involved may undertake deliberate unification. This means entrusting elite leadership to persons who have little interest in penalizing opponents and who will establish procedural safeguards that protect elite persons (and others) from undeserved and ruinous penalties. The elitist paradigm's essential message that elites are inevitable in all developing and developed societies, and that stable, representative political institutions cannot exist without an internally secure and trusting body of elite persons, may facilitate elite unifications.

Thus factional leaders in countries with disunified elites who understand the paradigm are obligated to do what minor things they can to protect themselves and their associates in political struggles and to restrict the successes of their opponents. But they must not carry these obligations to the point of inhibiting tendencies that could lead to a consensual, or even an imperfect, elite unification. In addition, they should certainly eschew all actions that would facilitate the imposition of an ideological unified elite.

Is it reasonable to expect that ideological unified elites might also move deliberately towards a consensual unity? Possibly in the long run it is. The inspiration and sense of mission that derive from a single, imposed ideology fade out in the course of two generations at most in such elites. First the Russian elite, and now lately the Chinese, have succeeded in making their own positions considerably less risky by eliminating the severe penalizations and by reducing the widespread scapegoating that characterized both of them during their early histories. Indeed, the positions and behaviour of Russian and Chinese leaders have always been fairly elitist when measured against the democratic, self-effacing political principles that have recently been widely professed among Western elites. Despite their official egalitarianism, in other words, these leaders already have a certain interest in the elitist paradigm. As those generations of Russian, Chinese and East European elites who have lived dangerously by wagering a narrow doctrine against history and sociology now pass from the scene, it is likely that succeeding generations will be more inclined to look for reasonable and safe settlements.

In time, if wars or really severe resource shortages can be avoided, an eventual mitigation of political conflicts and instabilities can be expected. The main problem is instilling prudence and patience over a long transitional period. Those who see the elitist paradigm's implications will aspire in common to avoid ideological positions that promise (and threaten!) to set the world right once and for all. There is reason to hope for a buffer of competent political representatives and managers, at first anonymous but eventually expressing the confidence that comes from shared common sense, to fend off the harbingers of Armageddon.

The elitist paradigm implies that a decent peace in a world that admits of no ideal solutions is a practical goal. But it also implies not pushing too hard for it, and not thinking that one has a simple mechanism for reaching it. In political life, there is only the constant give and take of rival goals. Thus adherents of elitism must refrain from advocating full equality because it simply cannot be arranged in any complex society. They must not presume that persons will act very often on the basis of high-cost altruism, for they will not. They must handle the occupational and class conflicts of developing societies with sophistication, focusing on the establishment of elite safety and trust. In developed societies, these adherents must deal with the conflicts between elites, insiders and outsiders by making sure, as far as is possible, that everyone has an opportunity to participate in useful but not heavily burdensome activities.

In sum, the political morality to be derived from the elitist paradigm frequently counsels inaction or extreme caution, even in the relatively safe atmosphere produced by a consensual unified elite. This should be no surprise to persons who are acquainted with the historically normal course of politics, as contrasted with the somewhat aberrant political conditions of recently affluent developed societies. Usually in politics too much is at stake and too many people are threatened by any given political tendency for innocents to become seriously involved. This remains the case today in most countries where disunified elites are present.

The decision to act politically in some new way is difficult for elites and non-elites alike. Most really important and helpful actions can originate only with persons who are strategically placed and influential, that is, with elites. But elites may choose not to act. Even where an elite is consensually unified some forms of injustice may prevail without there being any obvious ways of altering them. This is, of course, brutally true in a regime with an ideologically unified elite. Most of the time the ordinary citizen in the latter regime would be well advised to turn his back on any deliberate political innovation. Yet, over time even in this case, there is some basis for hope. For the most part, however, one must wait for elite initiatives to afford opportunities for constructive political action.

Chapter 5
Elites and the management of world problems

The most ominous longer-term world problems in the present period are of a kind that require steady, responsible and informed management. The general interdependence of nations through international trade has greatly diminished the scope for isolationist or autarchic policies. Consequently, there must be fairly constant negotiations between nations merely to keep essential channels of exchange open and to prevent the hostility of aggrieved peoples from disrupting the flow of resources that supports current development levels. Similarly, within nations there must be constant negotiations in order to contain increasingly forceful assertions of group interests that threaten to disadvantage less organized groups seriously and to make nations themselves dangerously vulnerable to international economic and political pressures.

Although they more frequently ramify through the entire world order, today's major international and national problems are still typical political problems in the sense that they admit of no solutions, only settlements. This is because there are no general moral standards to which all who are involved subscribe. Instead, all parties are confident of the rightness of their basic claims. At best, therefore, they can be persuaded to make only those concessions that are necessary to ward off the worst consequences of formal or informal warfare, whether international or civil. As we have stressed, this is always the nature of political settlements.

The details of the kinds of political settlements that are now required have to be negotiated over and over again. This requires much patience and careful attention by persons whose situations enable them to devote themselves fully and knowledgeably to this activity, namely elites. With respect to current world problems, merely asking people what they want or what they think is right, which is the essence of the democratic process, is a useless endeavour that risks exacerbating conflict. Instead, the complex ramifications of current world problems and their requirement for repeatedly negotiated settlements create an especial need for elite action.

Thus the tendency of the conflict between elites and insiders to restrict, even to paralyse, elite action in developed societies is in effect a world problem. In order to retain their power to negotiate settlements to international and national problems, elites must discourage excessive participation in decision-making by persons who have the time and the interest to dabble in it. This means that they must persuade the large, educated cadres of semi-professional and professional personnel in developed societies of the necessity for elite discretion in such matters. To do this, however, elites' confidence in their own legitimacy and consciousness of their own pivotal roles must be greater than they have recently been.

I

A major category of current international problems falls under the rubric of the North–South conflict. The 'North' consists of the developed countries. The 'South' consists of the less developed countries in the so-called Third World. As we shall show, the dynamics of this conflict closely resemble, and actually overlap, the insider–outsider conflict currently occurring within the developed societies.

The North–South conflict is the residue of five centuries of economic and political history. In the terms in which we conceptualized it in chapter 2, socioeconomic development began in earnest in the Low Countries and England during the late Middle Ages. It occurred first in these countries probably because large amounts of agricultural land came into the hands of persons who were in a position to treat it as an investment for profit. Rather than merely deriving a subsistence – generous for aristocrats, niggardly for peasants – from the land under their control, these owners were in a position to plan, calculate, and invest. Probably only capitalist owners of productive land can be expected to pursue economic efficiency by restricting the agricultural labour force to that which is strictly necessary.[1] But in any case, when such restriction was introduced a considerable body of labourers were turned loose and had to seek employment in incipient towns and cities. This in turn afforded a basis for capitalistic production in activities other than agriculture.[2]

An unplanned social revolution was thus set in motion in these countries and to some degree in near-by countries that were influenced by the examples of England and the Netherlands. Gradually developing into a large-scale economic system, capitalism afforded a basis for technological innovation, labour discipline and production and exchange that was rationally planned, at least from the standpoint of those who tended to control it. It immediately benefited considerable numbers of people, but by no means any large proportions of the populations involved. Eventually, however, the benefits of capitalist development became widespread within those West European countries that experienced it consistently and among Europeans who settled sparsely in resource rich areas outside Europe. By the late nineteenth century, for example, there could be little doubt that large majorities of these populations were substantially advantaged by the development that had taken place.

The existence of a 'core' area of countries that had seriously modernized and become more economically efficient had marked effects on other countries where more traditional production methods prevailed.[3] In a 'semi-periphery' of countries and territories (originally those adjacent to the core, i.e. France, Italy, Western Germany), conditions were somewhat similar to those in the core countries. In both core and semi-peripheral areas the

1 Why English and Dutch land-owners were inclined toward such rational, maximizing behaviour where and when they were is the subject of much debate (see R. Davis, *The Rise of the Atlantic Economies,* Cornell University Press, 1973; and I. Wallerstein, *The Modern World-System,* New York and London, Academic Press, 1974).

2 Whether economic 'efficiency' is beneficent depends on the relation of population to available resources. If there are too many people, the inefficiency of traditional village production systems may be preferable from the standpoint of the people involved. Yet economic efficiency in the form of refusing to pay more persons to work in a production process than are strictly necessary seems to have been crucial to socioeconomic development historically. It is not at all certain that development can take place without it.

3 We borrow the concepts of core, semi-periphery, periphery, and world system, as well as part of the general scheme for relating them, from I. Wallerstein, *op. cit.*

social change accompanying capitalist development tended to increase personal freedom on an actively individualistic basis.

Beyond the core and semi-peripheral countries, however, in a 'periphery' that extended as far into the rest of the world as the strong influence of the new system was felt, the effect was quite different. In this new 'world system's' first expansion during the sixteenth century, eastern Germany and the countries fronting on the Baltic further to the east were the periphery, or the extreme area affected by the system. Their established upper classes responded to opportunities for trade with the core and semi-peripheral countries by sharply repressing their populations and by reintroducing various forms of personal unfreedom. This enabled landlords to enter the emerging world market with inexpensive raw materials, especially foodstuffs, which they exchanged for products from the core and semi-periphery to their own considerable advantage.

As the world system expanded until it eventually became truly global, successive peripheries responded in similar fashion. That is, given low productivity and limited opportunities for actively individualistic freedom, there could be little profitable interaction with the more productive countries except as small circles in the peripheral areas were able to take advantage of their broad control over labour and resources. Trading with the more advanced countries was characterized by low prices for the peripheral countries' goods and by high prices for what the more developed countries offered in exchange. In many cases the greater military force of the latter gave them political leverage. Thus, the terms of trade necessarily developed to the advantage of the more economically and militarily efficient countries, while the gains to the less developed countries tended to be limited to their dominant upper classes. Over the five centuries during which this process occurred, the earliest semi-peripheral countries, together with new, sparsely settled countries such as the United States, Canada and Australia, eventually joined the core, the early peripheral countries became at least semi-peripheral, and new peripheral countries and areas steadily formed until the system became really world-wide about 1900.

In 1980, the core of the world system consists of the dozen or so countries, including Japan, that are generally called Western and developed. Nearly the entire populations of these countries must be seen as advantaged by the way in which socioeconomic development has occurred globally. The semi-periphery consists mainly of the countries of Eastern Europe. Except for a handful of oil-rich Middle Eastern countries, which appear to be moving rapidly toward semi-peripheral status, the remaining countries of Africa, Asia and Latin America are highly conscious of their peripheral status, although objectively the development of Latin American countries is considerably advanced over most other countries in the Third World, and many of them might therefore be considered semi-peripheral.

II

As a result of the way in which the world system expanded, peripheral and some semi-peripheral developing countries at present face Western developed countries with substantial grievances. The former were all brought into the system in ways that advantaged only limited proportions of their populations. As independent nations in the post-colonial world, they find their productivity, their income levels, their resources, and the terms of their trade distinctly disadvantageous as compared with the developed countries. For example, some 1,341 million people in especially low income African and Southern Asian countries have an average *per capita* income of US$152. Some 1,057 million people in the high income countries (essentially the United States, Australia, Canada, New Zealand, most of Europe and some oil-rich Arab states) have an average *per capita* income of about US$4,361. Latin American countries are mainly located in the intermediate category.[4]

One particularly ominous disparity is the increasing dependence of developing countries even in matters of subsistence. During the last fifteen years, the less developed countries have come to form a food deficit area because their population increases have outrun their increases in food production. Thus, *per capita* grain consumption averages 576 kilograms in the developed countries but only 220 kg in developing countries with market economies and 257 kg in developing countries with planned economies. The only

4 These and the succeeding data are from the 'Statistical Annexes' in J. W. Sewell, *The United States and World Development, Agenda 1977*, New York and London, Praeger, 1977, pp. 144–245.

substantial food surpluses are those of the United States, Canada, Australia and New Zealand. Since 1971, moreover, attempts to increase food production in most developing countries have been checked by a rapid increase in the cost of fertilizers which must be purchased from the developed countries. With the exception of petroleum, energy sources are also concentrated in the developed countries. While thirteen petroleum-producing countries, organized in OPEC, have since 1973 greatly increased the price that developed countries must pay for this resource, their action has had serious adverse consequences for the many developing countries that also import petroleum.

Many people in the less developed countries see these disparities as resulting from unfair advantages that developed countries obtained more or less fraudulently or forcefully, especially during long periods of colonial rule. Consequently, in recent years Third World countries have conducted a steady campaign, relying particularly on United Nations machinery, for better terms of trade, increased development subsidies, and a 'new world economic order'. They constantly demand tariff preferences, development aid grants, specially favourable borrowing terms, and the cancellation of outstanding debts.

If developed countries are to deal seriously with the developing nations some concessions in these areas obviously have to be made. Quite apart from moral, humanitarian considerations, the point has been passed where the developed world could stand aloof and simply refuse to treat with the Third World except on its own terms. This is because combining materials from all over the world is a fundamental feature of modern industrial processes. American industry, for example, is substantially dependent on the following imports from Third World countries: columbium 97%, tin 73%, fluorspar 67%, aluminium 63%, cobalt 50%, manganese 48%, mercury 38% and tungsten 36%. Given that the use of force in the old sense of colonial rule is now generally rejected, these import dependencies ensure that more or less constant negotiation with Third World countries is a necessity.

Yet substantial and dramatic concessions by developed countries in this negotiation are not likely to gain political support at home. Populations of the developed countries generally take the view that their favourable world market positions are not the result of sharp or unscrupulous practice, but are instead suitable rewards for having developed first. But even if this political restraint on the developed countries did not exist, merely yielding more of world income to the less developed countries could only moderate the North–South conflict to a very limited extent. Because of the population ratios involved, any substantial shift of income from the developed countries to the Third World would result in significant deprivations in the developed societies but would not significantly increase *per capita* well-being in the Third World.

As we have said, the insider–outsider conflict in developed societies between persons who have relatively secure occupational positions and those who are fairly strictly superfluous to the economies is very similar to, and in fact substantially overlaps, the North–South conflict. Not only are developing societies themselves increasingly outsiders in the world system's economy, but the culturally deprived, undeveloped, and economically superfluous sectors of their populations are in situations that closely resemble the situations of the outsiders in developed countries (what might be called 'internal underdevelopment' in the latter). In increasing degree, moreover, the ranks of outsiders in the developed countries actually consist of immigrants, frequently illegal, from the developing countries themselves.

This last trend is an inevitable result of the ratios between population, resources and income in the Third World. To the less fortunate components of Third World populations, even very poor employment opportunities in the developed countries at first look like good jobs. Wherever it is possible to do so, therefore, people move in steady streams from the developing to the developed countries. Because the land frontier between Mexico and the United States is essentially uncontrollable at any reasonable cost, the flow of illegal Latin American immigrants across it is constant and increasing. Most developed European countries have recently encouraged temporary immigrants from North Africa and the Middle East, not to speak of immigrants from the somewhat less developed countries on the northern rim of the Mediterranean, to take the kinds of inferior jobs which their own labour forces no longer accept. These temporary immigrants usually strive to become permanent. Even in such a remote area as Australia, the illegal arrivals of boatloads of refugees from South-East Asia threaten to contribute to the growth of the outsider category in that country.

To summarize, the dynamics of the North–South conflict closely parallel those of the insider–outsider conflict in developed societies. The largest part of the populations of developed societies are insiders, consuming a major part of the world's valued goods, and having assured access to resources far in excess of their proportionate share. All but small, privileged groupings of people in developing societies are outsiders, whose labour and skills are increasingly superfluous to the employment needs of the world economy and who therefore cannot aspire to much more than a subsistence living in the ballooning cities of the Third World. Although the ways in which this imbalance was created encourage outsiders to make vehement demands for concessions from the insiders, any simplistic redistribution, even if it were possible politically, would impose severe deprivations on the insiders while failing, because of the population ratios involved, to increase significantly the outsiders' living standards. Because this conflict cannot be adjudicated according to any clear principle, the expectation must be that it will long continue.

III

Partly reinforcing and partly cross-cutting the North–South conflict is another major conflict among the nations of the modern world. This is the division between communist and non-communist states. The twentieth-century communist movement is a product of the social revolutionary tendencies in Western thought that became widespread during the period when the West was militarily secure from conquest by forces from outside its own culture area. A variety of political sects or movements, all seeking drastic social change, formed, divided and re-formed during the nineteenth and early twentieth centuries. These were generally socialist or anarchist, and they occasionally drew localized followings from lower social strata, as well as from the intelligentsia. Espousing radical egalitarian and libertarian goals and values, they were seldom capable of firm organization, however, and they could never make any serious claims to success until the Russian Bolshevik faction came to power in 1917.

The Bolshevik success made manifest a change in the fortunes of radical causes. This may be attributed to an indirect, somewhat concealed shift to authoritarian and even hierarchical organization within the radical movement. It was probably not a fully conscious shift in the Bolshevik case or in the organizations in other countries that were prepared to affiliate with the Bolsheviks. However, it occurred through the practice of claiming special expertise in revolutionary matters for the members of a tightly-knit and exclusive organization that came to preempt the name 'party' from more loosely organized groups of adherents and supporters.

A body of specialized writings by Karl Marx and his followers, which purported to analyse the processes of historical change, had spread widely in revolutionary circles. It was this doctrine that the Bolshevik faction of the Russian Social Democratic Party, and subsequently the other national organizations affiliated with the world communist movement, claimed a special ability at expounding. The result was a change of emphasis in radical thinking. From the shared desire to mobilize mass movements for social change along egalitarian and libertarian lines, attention shifted to making systematically 'correct' decisions according to a doctrinal system that supposedly offered the key to revolutionary success. This allowed the emerging communist movement to begin a new trend in radical organization. A quasi-military pattern, which was in practice both authoritarian and hierarchical, replaced the more open, often crudely and naively democratic organizations to which social revolutionaries had previously belonged.

In its initial spread at the end of World War I, communism came into power permanently only in Russia. However, the Russian communists proceeded to draw sympathizers from within the socialist and social democratic parties throughout the world and to integrate them into a tightly knit world-wide organization. This was the Comintern, which consisted of many national communist parties. With the prestige that accrued to it from the seizure of the Russian state, international communism tended to absorb or forestall other vehement radical movements. In effect, Moscow had nearly a monopoly of serious, purportedly egalitarian revolutionary action for some forty years after the Russian Revolution. During this period, the residue of social radicalism in most countries settled into social democratic organizations. These were mainly anxious to differentiate themselves from the communists. Consequently, they stressed their adherence to democratic and legal procedures wherever possible.

During the inter-war period, a sharp hostility between Bolshevik Russia and the leaderships of Western societies prevailed, although the Russian regime was eventually recognized by other states and took some part in international diplomacy. Committed, however, to a world-wide overthrow of existing society and, in their view, only temporarily existing as one state among many, the Russian communists could not cultivate strictly normal relations with other countries.

The circumstances of World War II eventually forced the Soviet Union into an uneasy alliance with the Western Powers, however. This coalition's victory in the war placed most of Eastern Europe at the military disposition of the Russians. As a result, several European countries came under the control of their local communists who were, in turn, subordinate to the Russian leadership. Exceptions were Yugoslavia and Albania where local communist movements came into control independently of Russian military intervention. In Asia also, the Chinese communist movement independently defeated the Kuomintang regime on the mainland, a local communist movement gained control from the French in North Vietnam, and another local communist movement with a somewhat ambiguous allegiance as between the Russians and the Chinese took control of North Korea. While the necessary subordination of communists in these several countries to Russian power differed greatly, most competent observers assumed until well into the 1950s that communism remained a tightly organized, world-wide movement that was governed in its essentials by the leaders of the Russian state.

All these events established a sharp psychological division between the communist states, which claimed to issue from revolutionary processes that would later 'liberate' the entire world, and 'capitalist' countries that were characterized by private enterprise market economies and the social and political prominence of business owners and managers. Despite subsequent shows of varying degrees of independence from Moscow by communist regimes, their origins in supposedly Marxian social revolutions have continued to stand in the way of normal relations with the Western countries.

Throughout the post-war period, communist countries, especially Russia and China, but latterly also Cuba, have attempted to infiltrate and to lead the Third World. While this has helped maintain dissension between them and Western countries, especially the United States, their attempts have met with relatively little success. Probably if real social peace and substantial productivity had in fact been achieved in the communist countries they would have been more successful in these efforts. But prosperity for the manual working class and for most other occupational categories has been much more evident in the capitalist countries than in the communist ones. With the partial exception of Yugoslavia, moreover, all communist regimes have been highly repressive of divergent opinions within their populations. Consequently, the developed countries have necessarily comprised the model followed or aspired to by most persons who seek greater productivity and more modern conditions in the Third World. To a degree, the frustration among communists that their limited appeal to Third World countries creates has contributed to the persistence of doctrinal positions that in turn have made relations between communist and non-communist states difficult.

One aspect of this is the large point that the communist states make of having eliminated the capitalist economic system in their countries. Thus they all claim to have socialist economies while the economies of the developed countries are at most 'mixed' and contain many essentially capitalist features. Less because of their admiration for the actual economic performance of the communist states than because of the strong historical association of foreign capitalism with imperialistic exploitation, many Third World countries also profess to have, or at least to aspire towards, socialist economies.

What this amounts to in practice varies from country to country, however. Because there is little effort in the Third World to duplicate the dubious efforts of some communist countries to socialize agriculture, and because agriculture still bulks very large in nearly all Third World economies, there is in effect no general practice in the Third World that conforms to socialist economic principles. Nonetheless, there is an obvious advantage for the communist countries in dealing with Third World countries that also profess allegiance to socialism, and there is some disadvantage for developed countries, whose foreign trade is in the hands of capitalist firms.

More fundamentally, the unequal distribution of resources and terms of trade which underlie the North–South conflict assures sufficiently antagonistic relations between the Third World and Western developed countries to allow constant opportunities for communist infiltration or intervention in the former. As occasional spokesmen for Third World interests, and as radical agitators in Third World politics, the communist states regularly complicate the developed countries' relations with the Third World. This situation is bound to continue for at least another generation, and it contributes to the need for constant international negotiation and manoeuvre.

IV

Management of these major international conflicts is likely to be more difficult in the foreseeable, future than it has been in the recent past. This is because the world economy is now facing the apparent end of an epoch during which technological progress and the expansion of international trade steadily increased the material resources available for human consumption. Over the last five hundred years Western technological progress, generously fuelled by the wealth obtained through favourable terms of trade with the rest of the world, created new wealth and new forms of wealth that had previously been unknown.

Given this long experience of material progress, it is not surprising that the first signs of ecological difficulties and of impending shortages of energy and other resources about twenty years ago were largely dismissed. Most persons assumed, and many still assume, that technological innovation will overcome these shortages in the same way as previous material scarcities had been eliminated during recent centuries. But the fact that a steady succession of new techniques for exploiting the earth's resources has not yet exhausted them is no assurance that with continued technological progress such resource exhaustion will not occur. Although the doctrine of diminishing returns once played a prominent part in economic theory, Malthus's ultimately correct warning came at the wrong time. Its appearance at the very start of a century of agricultural improvement and manufacturing expansion helped to seduce many thinkers into abandoning a reasonably pessimistic outlook on the more general problem of development.

As we have indicated, the first stimulus to Western material progress was organizational, not technological. Putting land into the possession of enterprising and moderately well financed persons created the motivation to seek profits by investing only so much of the factors of production as might be strictly necessary. The people who were thereby prevented from using land for subsistence purposes became available for employment by other entrepreneurs in manufacture and trade. In addition to stimulating the more prudent assembly of productive factors, these organizational changes also afforded opportunities for technological innovation.

Improvements in transportation by sail and in the means of warfare were probably the most notable technological innovations during the fifteenth and sixteenth centuries. By rapidly bringing the resources of the Western hemisphere and of Asia into the European trading system, warfare and maritime transport were directly profitable as economic activities in those times. During the next two centuries, a linking of abstract science with the ingenuity of artisans and tradesmen laid a basis for the great production advances of the late eighteenth and nineteenth centuries in Europe and in European populations settled abroad. Steam power, following on wind power, markedly advanced production and transportation. The easy distribution of energy in the form of electricity further facilitated productivity. Finally the drawing and conversion of petroleum from the earth was the basis for a major new source of energy, mainly through the device of the internal combustion engine.

What faces the world in the last part of the twentieth century, however, is an impending shortage of energy sources at reasonable prices, especially a shortage of petroleum. Wind, steam from coal, electricity from steam and other sources, oil – these are the energy sources which facilitated the recent rise of material civilization in the West, and to a lesser degree in the world as a whole. It is possible that additional major energy sources can be added to this list in the future. But there is no reason to count on finding them at reasonable costs. For example, the engineering efforts to exploit nuclear energy seem to point to increasing, possibly prohibitive costs. Much coal still remains in the ground, of course, but as countries move to exploit it under the incentives of very high oil prices will its cost also rise beyond what most will be able to pay? Similar considerations relate to non-energy resources, particularly metals, which are essential to present production processes.

It is very likely, then, that there will soon develop a serious and widespread interest in conservation. This will involve assuring that resources and their products are distributed to those who show themselves most able to use them. This is likely to produce an even sharper conflict of interest between the Third World and the developed countries. But whether this does or does not eventuate, there is no longer any realistic prospect that a redistribution of wealth among nations, or a disproportionately greater increase in the wealth of developing countries will be facilitated by any significant increase in the availability of desired resources. Instead, the rivalries over existing resources will almost certainly become. more acute.

V

The room for manoeuvre and negotiation that elites must have if they are to manage these conflicts and rivalries is at present severely limited by the attitudes of educated non-elites in developing and developed societies. These attitudes are a residue of the Western countries' recent political and economic world dominance. Educated persons in developing countries tend to view the rise of Western dominance as a diabolical process that involved the systematic plundering of non-Western areas. Consequently, they press their elites to seek restitution. Many educated persons in developed countries, on the other hand, fundamentally doubt the legitimacy of their countries' privileged world positions because of their attachment to ideas of universal justice and because the rise of the West undoubtedly involved much injustice. Consequently, they press their elites to adopt conciliatory positions and to right historical wrongs when dealing with the Third World. Among these influential groupings in both kinds of societies there is little support for the probably correct view that Western development was the product of highly accidental and unlikely circumstances that no one deliberately brought about.

Generally labelled 'imperialism', especially by its critics and victims, the process by which the West secured a disproportionate share of the world's resources was without real historical precedent. In pre-modern times, conquerors often moved long distances and brought foreign peoples under their rule and exploitation. Once they did this, however, they invariably settled into their local advantaged situations as small ruling classes. After the passage of a generation or so, it made no conceivable difference to the conquered populations where the ancestors of these ruling classes had come from.

By contrast, no such assimilation of Westerners to the local populations they conquered seems to have occurred in the whole history of Western imperialism. Possibly a consciousness of Western technical and military superiority made the assimilation of Western rulers or settlers into any non-Western culture impossible. Or possibly the availability of relatively rapid communication and transport, initially by sailing ship, kept all wandering bodies of Westerners tied to their European home cultures.

Whatever the reason, Western imperialism followed two patterns. In one, a large body of Western settlers, eventually forming a stratified society by themselves, took over a non-Western territory, completely overwhelming the native population. The natives were absorbed into the lower strata of the new Western society, as in Latin America, or they were treated as a deprived hereditary caste with highly restricted rights and opportunities, as in Southern Africa, or they were swept aside into small reserved areas when they were not literally exterminated, as in North America and Australia.

The other pattern occurred in areas where the local population was numerous and the Western intruders few. In this case, no real Western settlement ever occurred. Instead, Westerners ruled politically and they dominated the economy, but only as temporary agents of home interests. Each generation of Westerners sought to return home in retirement. Their replacements came out regularly from the home country to perform functions or make fortunes, but nearly always tried to return home in their later years. It was in these cases that 'imperial' rule was most sharply felt and resented by the native populations.

One further difference between the conquests and exploitation of earlier historical periods and Western imperialism should be mentioned. At the time when Western expansion began there was no morality professed anywhere in the world under which the military conquest of the weaker by the stronger was regarded as inherently wrong. People who were conquered or who lost their territory were considered unfortunate, and they were often pitied. But those who conquered them were regarded as merely fortunate and not, inherently and regardless of circumstances, as wrongdoers.

During their imperial expansion, however, Western societies gradually adopted unprecedently high standards of social and political morality. Abstract rights to 'liberty', 'equality', 'justice' and other good conditions were widely professed on a universalistic basis. While many rationalizations of Western rule over foreign

peoples were advanced by those most involved in it, these rationalizations always co-existed uneasily with the more abstract, universal values to which Western societies were increasingly
committed. By the late nineteenth century, as a result, it was
difficult for many educated Westerners to justify their rule of
'colonies', and in fact a growing number of them disavowed and
condemned imperialism. As colonial peoples themselves absorbed
Western culture, moreover, they acquired the same abstract and
universal values under which their colonial statuses could only be
regarded as improper and wrong. To become a consistent and
effective foe of Western imperialism, in other words, one had to
absorb the ideal values of the West.[5]

There has been a long and arduous debate over whether Western countries benefited from imperialism. It is obvious that particular business interests and those Westerners who made
professional careers as colonial administrators and military officers
did benefit. However, the critics of imperialism emphasized the
normally very high budgetary costs of colonies to the ruling countries, and they pointed out that no individual imperial power
effectively monopolized trade with its colonies. A common conclusion was that imperialism did not pay. Probably an objective
demonstration of this is inherently impossible, however, because
the alternative situation, in which the Western conquerors had
stayed at home, cannot be specified in any detail. The same
difficulty arises, of course, when one seeks to evaluate the advantages and disadvantages which colonial peoples derived from
Western rule. With the recent moralistic condemnation of imperialism, in any case, a matter-of-fact appraisal has seldom been
wanted.

What seems fairly clear is that the West as a whole gained much
from its imperialism. Given the low state of technology and enterprise in most of the world several centuries ago, there is no
reason to suppose that colonial products would have reached
Europe in significant quantities without imperialist organization
and penetration. In the absence of such products, particularly
those of the tropics, it is inconceivable that material progress in
the West could have occurred on anything like its actual scale.

5 This discussion of the special historical character of Western imperialism and
   the moral ironies it involved owes much to John Plamenatz, *On Alien Rule
   and Self-Government*, London, Longmans, 1960.

Similarly, there is no reason to suppose that much Western-type production would ever have occurred outside the West without imperialism.

Eventually, of course, these gains to the West reached proportions that were counter-productive for the maintenance of the empires themselves. That is, greater prosperity in the home countries, larger numbers of attractive careers there, and the spread of egalitarian and hence anti-colonial values in both the home and colonial populations eventually made the costs of holding colonies exceed the benefits. As a consequence of the social evolution of both the West and its colonies, after World War II the Western countries were incapable of holding their colonies much longer. This was widely appreciated by informed persons at the time, although it took a series of events during the post-war years to precipitate the sudden liquidation of the main Western empires.

Once the Japanese surrendered in 1945, it was necessary to reorganize the immense area of the Philippines, South-East Asia, the Indonesian archipelago, the Malay peninsula and Burma, all of which had been under Japanese occupation. This area was outside the range of serious Russian influence at the time, and settlements were therefore carried out under policies adopted or accepted by the United States, the only other post-war superpower. The Philippines, to which independence had been promised by the United States before the war, was set up as an independent state in 1946, albeit with extensive military and economic ties to the United States. Britain took back Burma, the Malay peninsula and its other possessions in the area. The Dutch, however, were not permitted to continue what had become a large and conspicuous war to overcome resistance to their rule in Indonesia. China fell into civil war, and the early victory of communist forces excluded serious Western influence there.

France, which was the most delicate diplomatic problem for the United States in the simultaneous reorganization of Europe under American leadership, was allowed to attempt to restore its rule in Indochina by force. However, a civil war broke out between a nationalist and communist regime in the north and a conservative native regime in the south, which was backed by France. In 1954, France was decisively defeated and withdrew. Fearing a spread of Russian or Chinese communist influence, the United States assumed direct support of the South Vietnam regime. This support escalated into large-scale American warfare in Indochina by 1965.

With no firm settlement in sight, and under great popular pressure at home to terminate this war, the United States withdrew in 1973, and the regime it had supported collapsed under continued communist attack two years later.

During the early stages of these South-East Asian struggles, Britain reached the conclusion that further efforts to maintain its rule over India and Burma were unwise. The British therefore withdrew from both countries in 1948. India immediately split up into two states along religious lines: India and Pakistan. As early as 1950, therefore, a major portion of the Western colonial empires had been liquidated: the Dutch possessions in Indonesia, the American possession in the Philippines, and the greatest colony of them all, India.

British policy continued steadily along the path of getting rid of its empire before excessive exertions to keep it would be required. Britain released its widespread African holdings between 1957 and 1962. The white-ruled, already more or less independent colony of Rhodesia unilaterally declared its independence in 1965 rather than risk British imposition of political rights for its black population. Although the French had resisted decolonization more stubbornly than the British, political sleight-of-hand and subterfuge by General de Gaulle during the early years of his semi-dictatorship freed France of practically all its imperial commitments by 1962. Of the major Western imperial powers this left only Portugal which, under a long-lasting, reactionary dictatorship, clung to its large African territories in spite of substantial local rebellions until 1974.

It is difficult to overstate the psychological blow to Western self-esteem created by this rapid, historically almost instantaneous, liquidation of empire. Not much of this psychological reaction appeared on the surface. Apparently there was little worth talking about. Yet the sense of purpose and of historical importance that had attached to public, particularly governmental, leadership in the major 'powers' of Europe – Britain and France – was suddenly sharply attenuated.

There was no glory in this, even for those who had opposed empire and wanted its end. To be sure, the British gained some satisfaction from having moved fast enough to salvage somewhat better relations with their former subjects than might have been expected. But for all informed West Europeans the decolonization process was too rapid and headlong to be interpreted as anything but a show of sudden weakness. Inevitably, the world role and significance of Europe suddenly dwindled, even in the eyes of the European countries that had not had colonies.

The crisis atmosphere in which these liquidations of empire were carried out left no time to prepare native elites and sub-elites for their new leadership roles. It was pointless to ask the somewhat patronizing question of whether particular native populations were ready for self-government. For the most part, they were not ready to maintain political regimes that Westerners would approve of, and Western forms of representative government seldom persisted more than a few years after independence.

Even for the United States, which had posed as an opponent of empires, and whose own direct imperial role had been confined mainly to the Philippines, the collapse of Western imperialism involved a great trauma. In part this was the general sense of uncertainty that arose from the entrance of half a world of new nations on the diplomatic stage. But more importantly, it was the specific disaster of American intervention in Vietnam after the collapse of French power in Indochina. For ideological reasons, the American public never saw this intervention as a belated colonial venture, even if this was how it was seen by much of the world. In the United States the Vietnam intervention was originally and always mainly seen as help given to people who presumably felt threatened by communist expansion in the same way as help was given to West European populations who feared Russian expansion.

The failure of American intervention in Vietnam was therefore a serious blow to American self-understanding and self-esteem. Historically, it was the first obvious defeat of United States forces in warfare if one took a simplistic view of wars and their outcomes, as many Americans were still inclined to do. This occurred at the very time when the United States had emerged as indisputably the leading military power in the world. Because it was largely incomprehensible in terms of American preconceptions, and because it could not be accepted as signalling a permanent and general loss of power and influence, the psychological trauma of this 'defeat' may have been more pervasively damaging than the sudden liquidation of empires had been for European populations.

VI

The widespread tendency among educated persons in Western countries to view the relatively ignominious circumstances in which the United States withdrew from South-East Asia as a case of 'just deserts' epitomizes the seriously deficient character of prevailing attitudes toward world problems in these countries today. Such persons are quick to label the economic and political involvements of Western countries in the Third World as 'neo-colonial', apparently on the assumption that only arrangements that recompense developing countries for their past and present disadvantages are to be tolerated. These same persons are widely prepared to view the endemic political instability of Third World regimes as a consequence of 'de-stabilization' programmes undertaken by capitalist interests in league with the intelligence operatives of the developed countries. There is, in short, a marked inclination to attribute the economic and political difficulties and disadvantages of the developing countries almost wholly to past and present evils perpetrated against them by the West.

As we have tried to suggest, this inclination arises much less from an objective appraisal of the causes and consequences of Western imperialism than from the kinds of assumptions and beliefs that imperialism fostered in the increasingly well-off populations of the imperial powers. Thus there is in these populations an inability to realize that they think and feel as they do *only* because they have enjoyed largely satisfying life circumstances, particularly in youth, and because they have come to take these circumstances so much for granted that they lack all conscious fear of losing them.

Accordingly, a substantial portion of Western populations does not recognize that they and the rest of the human race have a fundamental selfishness and only a limited capacity for altruism. Instead, they tend to suppose that all persons are essentially good neighbours, as they see themselves to be. They wish to treat really disadvantaged and demoralized peoples as political and social comrades, siding with them in their inevitable clashes with authority and privilege. Rather than forcibly resisting demands that cannot be expediently granted, they favour making concessions to whoever asks for them on the mistaken ground that such yielding reliably assuages grievances, as indeed it often does among strictly intimate and mutually empathetic persons.

It is more than a play on words that when these attitudes guide the assessment of the world problems we have discussed they are distinctly unworldly. Effective management of these problems thus requires that the educated cadres of developed countries unlearn enough of their unworldliness so that they can see their own situations more accurately, that is, as a well-disposed but privileged – and in considerable measure well-disposed *because* privileged – segment of world society. Once they recognize that the values that they seek to uphold can only be seriously realized amidst reasonably prosperous, politically stable conditions, the educated cadres of developed societies will presumably conclude that their societies are worth preserving at almost any cost.

Only when this conclusion becomes widespread is there a chance that elites in developed countries will be allowed the discretionary powers that are required to negotiate settlements of world conflicts and rivalries effectively. Furthermore, only when the educated cadres of developed societies are seen to support such elite action will it become apparent to influential strata in the Third World that the Western countries will not bow to vehement, restitutive demands and threats. This, in turn, will relieve some of the pressure on the elites of Third World countries to make unrealistic demands, thereby enabling them to bargain for settlements that are not harmful, and may even be marginally favourable, to their countries' interests.

The key to the management of the world's major problems, then, is recognition by well-off and well-intentioned persons in the West that their societies have a special worth. This involves seeing that they have conferred on a uniquely large number and proportion of people material, social, and aesthetic satisfactions of a high order, as well as a large degree of protection from the harsher vicissitudes of normal life, particularly inter-personal violence. To be sure, these benefits have always been partly offset by the poverty, insecurity and indignity that significant categories of Western populations have suffered. But these less personally successful and less socially favoured categories do not appear to have been worse off in Western countries than similar and proportionately much larger categories have been in all other urbanized civilizations. It is virtually certain, in other words, that the West shows a net superiority over all known civilizations in the number of persons to whom it has accorded at least moderate satisfaction.

Thus to justify efforts to preserve Western countries in their current conditions at almost any cost, one needs only to be reasonably sure that other countries in the world today could not be expected to equal or surpass these Western achievements if they did not have Western countries to contend with. For the reasons we have put forward, we think it most unlikely that the other countries of the contemporary world could do this. The way in which socioeconomic development occurred in the West was sufficiently fraught with historical accident as to make its occurrence again in other parts of the world highly unlikely. Indeed, the grossly disproportionate ratios of population to resources in most other countries virtually ensure that it could not.

It is only in the developed, affluent Western countries, moreover, that any large number of persons are individually carriers of Western values in their specific and subtle details. And it is largely only in these countries that one finds the elite structure and the institutional stability without which large numbers of people cannot have either the security for social benevolence or the opportunity for meaningful participation in social and political decision-making that are the essence of Western values and ideals. In any reasonable view of historical contingencies, therefore, Western civilization, once lost, would probably never be seen again, nor would anything much like it.

Chapter 6
Elitism: answers and questions

When a new paradigm is introduced, it must do two things if it is to be useful. First, it must suggest answers to problems that have previously proved baffling. Second, it must point to a variety of questions that could not be framed effectively without it and that seem to offer new avenues to knowledge. We believe that the elitist paradigm, as we have restated it, does both these things.

The paradigm offers a substantial explanation of one problem that has previously had no satisfactory solution. This involves the reason for the failure of democratic representative government to spread in the world during this century in spite of the general favour it has enjoyed in influential circles. The paradigm explains this by pointing to the dependence of institutionally stable government, a substantial degree of public freedom, and hence any meaningful form of representative democracy, on the existence of a consensual unified elite. It holds, in other words, that the occurrence of representative democratic government requires the following sequence of *necessary* conditions:

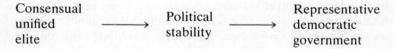

The elitist paradigm bases this causal explanation on a general conception of politics. This is that consensus about major political issues that directly affect the distribution of valued things is never deep nor widespread among non-elites. Once such issues rise to public consciousness, the tendency of non-elites is toward civil strife. Politics consists of the organization and use of coercive power to play out or to contain this tendency. Political stability is therefore never the result of all social actors co-operating voluntarily, peacefully and with adequate information. Instead, it is always the artificial product of a continued series of shrewd decisions made by those who are influential and politically active, that is, by elites.

Where elites are essentially trusting of each other, they are able to guide and direct the raising of political issues without allowing these to become deeply divisive. Only where such an elite exists are stable, representative political institutions possible. Even then, however, universality of representation (i.e., democracy) may require other facilitative conditions such as general economic well-being and the absence of highly exacerbated cultural cleavages.

The paradigm explains that the absence of consensual unified elites has made representative democracy impossible in most Latin American and other developing countries, in spite of many sincere attempts to institute it. By the same token, it explains that the presence of this kind of elite in countries such as Great Britain, the United States, the Netherlands and Sweden has fulfilled this necessary condition for political stability and representative government. In this way, the paradigm gives elite behaviour and structure a decisive role in the explanation of major political variations between and within societies.

The paradigm also shows how elite actions are limited and checked by non-elite configurations in different kinds of societies. Thus it explains that when elites have to seek popular support, as they usually do, they must tailor their policies and appeals to fit the non-elite orientations that arise from the composition of the work force. It shows how work force composition and non-elite orientations have changed historically and how this helps to explain the occurrence and non-occurrence of such dramatic political events as levelling and fascist revolutions and the rise of totalitarian regimes at different levels of socioeconomic development. As well, it shows how this change has limited the ability of disunified elites to undertake their own deliberate unification once non-elite categories became seriously mobilized and seriously divergent in their orientations.

Second, the paradigm allows the raising of many new questions that seem to point toward significant increases in useful knowledge. Perhaps the most important of these questions are the following: Can there be a general strategy for producing consensual unified elites in countries that now lack them? Is the further development of countries that are currently less developed to be generally expected, or is such development likely to be a relatively rare occurrence? If development occurs, to what extent will the political conflicts that it generated in earlier cases of successful development be repeated? More specifically, during current and future passages through the middle levels of development what will be the effect of the comparatively smaller proportion of manual workers in automated industries and of the correspondingly larger proportion of persons who are unemployed or precariously employed in urban service activities? In today's developed societies and in other societies that are nearing the developed condition, what can be done to prevent further increases in the size of the outsider category and to reintegrate its members into national life? Finally, what broad philosophical changes are needed to restore political realism to public discourse in Western and other societies?

In this concluding chapter, we shall outline some of the matters that will have to be investigated in order to answer these new questions. Pending such investigation, however, the merits of the elitist paradigm should be judged by the significance of the answers it gives to old questions and by the promise contained in the new questions it raises.

I

Elite disunity, political instability and recurrent dictatorial rule have characterized most societies throughout history. The elitist paradigm's implication that the presence of a consensual unified elite is necessary for institutional stability and, hence, for all the better features of political rule, thus seems to suggest a dismal political prospect for most developing countries today. For the person holding liberal values, it is frustrating to realize that historically such an elite has been attained only in rare and somewhat accidental circumstances. On the other hand, the novelty of the paradigm's causal linkage between elite consensus and unity, political stability and representative democratic government means that no serious thought has so far been devoted to this problem. Possibly, by giving such thought to the problem ways to transcend the historically normal form of politics can be found.

Let us suppose a world in which elites generally have grasped the paradigm's meaning. Would there then be improved prospects for the consensual unification of disunified elites? The fact that consensual unity enhances the security of elite persons and tends to give them more reliable collective influence on major political decisions suggests that disunified elites who understand the paradigm might be motivated to seek consensual unification. The question would be whether they could capitalize on circumstances that are propitious for such unification or even bring about such circumstances by deliberate measures.

Where there are only a few elite factions and they have recognized leaders, and where those factions and leaders are relatively isolated from non-elite pressures, an understanding of the paradigm might indeed prompt disunified elites to abandon their enmities in the same sudden way that English elites did in 1688–9. This would involve compromising on matters of principle in the fashion of Tory leaders who dethroned a king and appointed his successor, and of Whig leaders who accepted Episcopalianism as a privileged religion in the Settlement of 1689. In other words, recently warring elite factions might deliberately disassociate themselves from their previously intransigent positions in order to secure each other's support as a means of avoiding further serious conflict and of staying in power.

In most contemporary societies, however, there is a more complex elite division involving more complicated organizations of non-elites than existed in England during the late seventeenth century. In these circumstances, elite unification involves finding a way to bring different elite factions together on central policy questions while retaining the support of non-elite groupings. As it did in Norway and Denmark during the 1930s, this might involve a combination of policies that have some practical equalizing effects at the same time that they constitute a retreat from the more extreme challenges to existing status distributions.

Alternatively, elite unification in more complex circumstances might involve the rapid subordination of previously divisive class-based conflicts to a sort of ethnic or regional politics that cuts across class lines, involving ethnic camps emotionally without leading to any very sweeping actions. The turning of the tables as between the two linguistic divisions in Belgium in the early 1960s illustrates this mode of unification. Once the political predominance of the Flemings was clear, political conflicts became embedded in essentially detailed, although emotionally charged, ethnic issues such as the relocation of the University of Louvain and the definition of the rights of Francophones spilling over from Brussels into the surrounding Dutch-speaking area. This new issue largely blotted out the highly divisive social class issues that first seemed to be raised by the liberation of the Congo in 1960. Although Belgian elites presumably acted with little deliberateness in this redefinition of issues and conflicts, the Belgian case suggests how elites that are intent on greater unity might disengage themselves from positions that have previously locked them in conflict.

In Belgium, Norway and Denmark the unifications to which we have alluded occurred in elites that were already imperfectly unified. Moreover, they occurred in the context of parliaments and other representative political institutions that were comparatively stable. This was because right-of-centre elites in these countries had long demonstrated their control over reliable electoral majorities. Consequently, Belgian, Norwegian and Danish elites had at their disposal generally accepted parliamentary and other institutional procedures that enabled antagonistic factions to block their opponents' more radical policy initiatives and that helped each elite faction to conceal the modifications it made in its own more radical programmes. In these ways, representative institutional contexts facilitated elite unification in these countries.

In most developing countries today, however, elites are disunified rather than imperfectly unified, and, consequently, there are no seriously representative institutions that are already comparatively stable. Probably in much of Latin America and in most of the rest of the Third World political institutions are now too demonstrably unstable to justify any attempt at elite unification under the kind of institutional aegis that was available to Belgian, Norwegian and Danish elites. This suggests that in countries like Argentina or Peru it may be necessary for an essentially military elite to co-opt bureaucratic, professional, business, trade union and other sector leaders into decision-making processes while still retaining the essentials of a dictatorship. If a genuine condition of trust and of give and take could be established between such leaders even under openly oligarchical arrangements, then limited and controlled steps toward workable representative institutions might gradually become possible.

To summarize, in some countries with disunified or imperfectly unified elites consensual unification might be brought about through relatively open compromises among existing elite factions. In other countries some changes in elite personnel might be a necessary step in the unification processes. It is difficult to speak generally of the kind of somewhat unprecendented actions that are involved. But it seems likely that with the elitist paradigm's clear definition of the problem elite ingenuity might well find paths to consensus and unity under widely varying conditions.

II

To what extent is the further development of today's less developed societies likely? Oddly, in the whole widely ramifying discussion of development during the past thirty years, this question has not been seriously raised. There has instead been an extremely widespread tendency merely to affirm that these societies *must* develop. Apparently, the possibility that Western populations may remain prosperous while Third World populations continue to live in obvious misery far into the future has simply been an intolerable thought for the morally sensitive Westerners who have dominated the discussion of development. Yet, there is no inherent plausibility in the idea that many less developed countries will now, in a short period of time, accomplish what the countries of the original West took some five centuries to carry out.

Our paradigm raises this question because it indicates that further development by today's less developed societies will require managing non-elite conflicts that are significantly different from those that Western countries successfully managed during their own development. Already there are signs that these somewhat different conflicts may prove to be unmanageable.

Historically, passage through the middle levels of development involved the transfer of surplus agricultural and artisan workers to large numbers of manual industrial jobs, and to a growing number of substantial service occupations. As prosperity increased, moreover, an ever larger proportion of populations was supported in comfortable and honorific dependency statuses, such as housewives, tertiary-level students, pensioners and persons disabled physically or psychologically in various ways. Except during temporary economic downturns, this enabled the societies that industrialized early to avoid the problems of large-scale unemployment and underemployment until development was more or less completed.

In terms of the elitist paradigm, it is obvious that the tendency to borrow capital-intensive and labour-saving production techniques from the countries that developed first puts today's less developed countries in a quite different situation. Whereas large-scale manual employment was compatible with nineteenth-century production techniques, it is incompatible with today's techniques. This means that, even if they had no population explosions, less developed societies would be much less capable of absorbing surplus agricultural and artisan personnel into other parts of their work forces than were the countries that developed earlier. Not only are their industrial manual work force components small by historic measures, but these countries also lack the prosperity with which to support many persons in comfortable and honorific dependency statuses.

Most Third World countries still have large bodies of persons employed in subsistence agriculture, in low-paid and old-fashioned artisanship, and in a highly precarious set of service occupations, including domestic service. For these countries there is no prospect that further modernization, in and of itself, will solve their unemployment problems or even alleviate them. Rather, the impending prospect is of a rapid growth of an outsider category whose members contemplate entry into the regular employment market with incredulity.

It is difficult to foresee the detailed social and political ramifications that large outsider categories will have in less developed societies. Because they perform few, if any, really needed tasks in the work force, outsiders lack the occupational leverage and concrete interests that industrial working classes and other work force components had in the historical cases of Western development. This probably means that the actions of outsider categories will depend to a large extent on local cultural tendencies. Where cultural traditions remain viable, as for example in some Islamic countries, they could readily lead to widespread discontent and to an eventual choking off of the willingness to copy Western methods.

Even where cultural traditions do not result in sharply anti-Western movements among outsiders, there is no certainty that any real Westernization, as measured by widespread bureaucratic and technological sophistication, will occur in most of the now less developed societies. This is because there appears to be no reliable way to recreate the highly effective system of motivations that led to large-scale transformations of Western populations from tradition-following peasants to calculators of means to ends and of ways of individually getting ahead.

In the West this process involved brutal measures, and it is in order to prevent a repetition of these that most less developed countries have chosen to follow socialist or quasi-socialist development strategies. Yet, it is by no means certain that these strategies contain sufficient motivations for individual persons to discard traditional and fatalistic orientations and thereby to transform society. For what it is worth, Marx and Engels clearly did not think so. They saw capitalistic exploitation, centring on the aggrandizing activities of capitalist entrepreneuers, as an effective and necessary means of increasing productivity. They believed that only after high productivity had actually come about could socialism be introduced in order to achieve a less brutal, more fair and equal distribution of wealth and status.

Within the elitist paradigm, therefore, the question of whether further development of many less developed countries is likely must be treated as open. Not only is it unclear that the kind of elites that would operate stable political institutions can be created, but it is also unclear that the problem of surplus labour can be contained and managed so as to allow development to proceed. Even if solutions to these difficulties can be found, there is still reason to ask whether the motivational mechanisms that are seemingly essential to development can be instilled in many less developed societies.

III

In chapter 2 we indicated that unemployment and underemployment in developed societies tends to be concentrated in social groups that are in one way or another unprepared for, or disinclined toward, the limited employment vacancies that are available in these societies. Ethnic groups that have recently immigrated or that have been steadily discriminated against come to doubt their ability to conform to required employment standards. Youths brought up in cultivated leisure either want no employment at all, or they want the kind of 'meaningful' jobs that cannot be multiplied sufficiently to satisfy the numbers who seek them. As women increasingly reject their former honorific dependency statuses, but still retain their traditional responsibilities for housework and childcare, many find themselves in outsider positions as welfare recipients or persons precariously employed in low-paid and low-status jobs.

These are some of the factors that cause particular groups of persons to flow into the outsider category of the unemployed or the casually employed. However, these factors do not account for the scope of unemployment in developed societies. This is the result of objective changes in the kinds and numbers of jobs that are strictly needed for the type of work that is deemed necessary and useful in these societies.

Contrary to the assumptions underlying much government policy, there can be no remedy for this general problem along the lines of retraining individuals and attempting to modify the pattern of skills or the emotional inclinations of the particular groups now caught or threatening to be caught in outsider statuses. Only some fairly fundamental change in the basis for justifying jobs can meet the problem of the outsiders as a category.

The best clue to what has to be done is the way in which the early manifestations of surplus labour were abated and retarded during World War II and the Cold War that followed it. The national defence industries that nearly all the developed societies operated during this period obviously created employment without much regard to the demand for its material products. Weapons systems had to be provided at appropriate levels of sophistication even though the countries producing them during the Cold War period usually had the good fortune of not using them and of merely replacing them when obsolete. Large military forces had to be kept in a state of preparedness even though the prospect of their actual deployment in warfare was fairly remote. In this way, many persons were usefully employed at essentially precautionary tasks. Their work was intended to ward off an unsatisfactory outcome, military defeat. In this sense their work was as useful if no serious warfare occurred as it would have been if it contributed to a successful defence after the outbreak of war.

The example of defence activity illustrates a major aspect of much service employment. This is the difficulty of justifying such employment according to the productivity measures that are normally used to evaluate methods for producing material goods. Like a defence industry, much service employment is simply designed to prevent certain things from happening. Thus by his presence a policeman prevents the commission of some crimes. By practising his profession, an auditor prevents a certain number of attempts to defraud firms. Like a soldier in peacetime, a fire-fighter has not been uselessly employed during a period in which no fires occur.

It is conceivable, of course, that the onset of more pressing needs for national defence than are now obvious may enable some or all developed societies to make major inroads against the grow-ing numbers of permanently unemployed and underemployed per-sons in their populations. It is also conceivable that the proliferation of serious ecological and pollution problems may allow many currently unemployed persons to be employed at essentially precautionary tasks. However, these and similar event-ualities would comprise *accidental* abatements of the outsider problem in developed societies, just as World War II and the Cold War accidentally interrupted the early manifestations of this problem.

Is there a less fortuitous way of meeting this problem of out-siders? Can one calculate the actual need for useful employment in a developed society's population and then create enough jobs of a precautionary and preventive character to reverse current unemployment trends? The elitist paradigm defines the question clearly, but it does not as yet give a clear answer. Instead, by emphasizing the determinant importance of concrete work roles and interests for non-elite behaviour, it counsels scepticism when evaluating proposals merely to 'make' work for people by dividing up and sharing jobs between two or more persons, by funding national service programmes that would employ entire age cohorts in 'clean-up' activities, and the like.

Merely creating simple, ineffective or useless jobs in order to avoid paying the unemployed for doing nothing would be point-less. This is because no avowedly 'make work' scheme can possibly avoid the evasions of workers who are ill-disposed to perform useless tasks for a pittance or the consequent resentments of taxpayers who would quickly notice these evasions. To solve the outsider problem in a deliberate, rather than an accidental, way, it is strictly necessary to create real jobs in the sense of jobs that would require substantial qualifications for which persons could then be specifically trained.[1]

1 Cf. G. L. Field, 'Work, responsibility and service occupations', *Phi Kappa Phi Journal*, 57 (1977), no. 1, pp. 54–62.

IV

In contemplating national and international problems, elites and other politically attentive persons in Western societies are still strongly influenced by the deceptive and unrealistic ideas that are a residue of the West's recent circumstances. These centred on the military invincibility of the West as a whole and on the tempting but elusive prospect of overcoming inequality by overcoming material scarcity in Western populations. As these circumstances recede, the ideas that they helped make speciously convincing will also recede. Presumably, Western elites and their supporters will again become accustomed to the historically usual need to defend the material and cultural acquisitions of their 'own people', however they might be defined, against the avoidable incursions of others.

When this happens, Western leaders will come to see their current benevolent and altruistic aspirations to reshape the rights and privileges of the world's peoples as foolish. They will realize that their power to transform other societies is very slight and that the costs of attempting such transformations are heavy. Just as Western societies (including Japan) are no longer capable of imperial rule, so they are no longer sufficiently entrenched to play the role of world benefactors. To be sure, they still have substantial technological advantages over other societies. But through bad luck or through continued self-deceptions a time could easily come when Western societies would have no individual or collective alternative but to pay immense blackmail to a set of militant, but culturally traditionalist, new powers that would be frustrated in their own efforts at development except for the borrowings of advanced weaponry.

While the adoption of more realistic ideas is bound to occur among the elites and educated cadres of Western societies, it is quite conceivable that it could occur too late to save some significant part of Western civilization. Thus there is a compelling need to change the content and mood of intellectual life in these societies more deliberately and rapidly. The first requirement for this change is to reconstitute a sense of self and other, especially with respect to the way in which elite and other moderately influential persons think of themselves and their roles. As we have stressed previously, a more self-consciously elitist frame of reference is one of the things that is needed if Western elites and their supporters are to stem internal conflicts involving insiders and outsiders, as well as manage conflicts between developed and developing societies. Recognition of the need for such a frame of reference has been conspicuously absent in Western intellectual and cultural circles in recent decades. To create it, some of Western intellectual history over the last two or three centuries has to be retraced.

Three aspects of modern Western philosophical development are at the root of the problem. The first is the neglect of the naturalistic conclusions of Machiavelli and Hobbes about human motivation. The second is the rise of the value-free position in social science. The third is the consequent possibility to assert, from time to time, the categorical imperative of Kant, as well as similar altruistic and allegedly objective value positions.

The sequence has been something like the following. With Machiavelli and Hobbes Western speculative philosophy came down flatly in favour of a world-view that omitted entirely the objective idea of values as obligatory for all. The ancient philosophers had supported this idea by urging that personal contemplation could reveal such values. Subsequently, however, greater philosophical maturity had made this untenable for worldly thinkers. But in the meantime, the idea of objective and obligatory universal values received important support for at least a millenium and a half from the fact that the profession of Christian belief was more or less compulsory.

The essence of the position developed by Machiavelli and Hobbes was a value relativism in which the only value that could be used meaningfully in the analysis of human affairs as they actually occurred was that based on the more or less enlightened self-interest of individual actors or cohesive groups. This amounted to saying that, if the chips are down, the individual person and *a fortiori* the organized group to which he belongs will not prove capable of high-cost altruism. Nations, classes, interest groups and individuals will, so far as they may realistically do so, cling to, or seek, advantages even at serious cost to other nations, classes, interest groups and individuals. This does not deny that altruistic conduct will sometimes be possible in the case of individuals or small groups who are tightly integrated into larger social units. Indeed, such individuals or small groups may well die to preserve their own people when the alternative would be disgrace,

annihilation, loss of culture or enslavement. But, unless compelled, they will not make serious sacrifices for strangers.

This is an essentially sound position and one that is highly
relevant to the problems of contemporary political and social
order. In fact, until after World War II it appeared to be largely
accepted in the social analysis carried out by elite persons,
although it was seldom clearly formulated. With respect to the
functioning of elites it means that there are always matters of
dispute that they should not throw open to public argument or
democratic decision-making. Yet this position is awkward to
explore without seeming to threaten many people, and it is, of
course, a shocking position to those who profess a universally
binding morality of a religious nature. Indeed, in earlier centuries,
when the force of Christian belief was much greater than it is
today, there was a strong incentive to avoid too close an identi-
fication with this position. Thus both Machiavelli and Hobbes
have always had a limited audience, although this was by no
means only because they inspired genuine disbelief.

The optimism of the Enlightenment, and subsequently that
based on the advances of science and technology and the concom-
itant growth of Western power during the nineteenth century,
created a way of avoiding the open profession of value relativism.
This escape was the value-free position which permeated social
science and, indeed, social thought in general.

As we noted in prefacing this book, until recently advances in
the physical and life sciences afforded no obvious threats to human
well-being. Rather, it was generally assumed that any such
advances would only contribute to greater human happiness. Since
these established sciences were thought to be value-free, that is,
since they were generally discussed in a context that lacked overt
value discrimination, why should not the same practice be followed in the discussion of social matters? In the prevailing atmosphere of scientific and technological advance it was difficult to
see any increase in knowledge as obviously threatening. But probably more important, adopting the value-free position enabled the
social scientist, and even the statesman, to avoid open debate
about values and thus to avoid either the embarrassment of clearly
sponsoring a selfish conception of human nature, *à la* Hobbes, or
of having to appear naïf in defending the moral evaluations of
established religion.

Obviously, it was never the case that politicians, administrators, and social scientists actually took no value positions. On occasion they strongly advocated value positions that were generally acceptable to the audiences they addressed. In fact, it is impossible to participate in politics and, as the verbal jibberish in which many ostensibly value-free social scientists indulge shows, it is difficult even to discuss politics from a strictly value-free position. Nevertheless, it was possible for those who were well placed in the optimistic atmosphere of the nineteenth and the first two-thirds of the twentieth centuries to ignore serious and difficult value questions. Precisely because of this, there was no barrier in standards of sophistication to prevent the introduction of utterly simplistic value commitments and exhortations whenever it appeared appropriate and noncontroversial to do so. Thus only the accumulated human wisdom transmitted in the ideologies of liberalism and socialism served to keep the conduct of elites fairly realistic. But all the while the absence of any direct concern with serious normative philosophy facilitated the frequent expression of altruistic positions like Kant's categorical imperative that purported to apply universally and objectively and that, as values, were in fact foreign to the empirical and scientific attitudes of the age.

Once liberalism and socialism were supplanted by the vacuous and naive platitudes of welfare statism after World War II, it became a distinct possibility that elites would not merely utter these platitudes but would actually trust them to describe and predict the actual conduct of persons and groups. To a considerable extent, this has now come to pass. Thus it is to combat such naive tendencies and to stop the growing escalation of the future confrontations to which they are leading that elites in the developed societies desperately need to reconstitute a self-consciously elitist frame of reference.

Index

Africa: and democracy, 58; and elite structure, 50; end of empires in, 112; instability, 36, 50; *per capita* income, 99; as periphery, 99
Argentina, and elite unification, 121
Asia: and democracy, 58; and elite structure, 50; and ideological unified elites, 74; instability, 36, 50; *per capita* income, 99; as periphery, 99
Australia: consensual unified elites, 38, 50; illegal immigrants, 101; imperialism in, 109; *per capita* income, 99–100; socioeconomic development, 29–30, 98
Austria: disunified elite, 50; fascist regime, 29; suppression of liberal practices in, 49

Belgium: consensual unified elite, 120–1; ethnic division, 86–7, 89; imperfectly unified elite, 40, 50, 73, 120; socioeconomic development, 29–30; suppression of liberal practices in, 49
Bell, D., 24n
Bolsheviks, 102–3
Brinton, C. B., 28–9, 36
British Labour Party, 8, 10
bureaucracy: and elites, 71–2; and power, 70–1
Burma, 111–12

Canada: consensual unified elite, 38, 50; ethnic division, 86, 88–9; *per capita* income, 99; socioeconomic development, 28–30, 98
China (People's Republic of): communism in, 104, 111; ideological unified elite, 36, 92–3; possible elite consensus and unity, 92–3; and Third World, 104
Clark, C., 24n

class, 31–4
Cold War, 30
Comintern, 103
communist states: conflict with non-communist states, 102–6; political repression in, 105; and social democracy, 103; and Third World, 104–6
consensual unified elites: concept of, 36–9; creation of, 76–8, 92–3, 118–22; and democracy, 37, 57, 117–18; and developed societies, 41; and discrimination, 82–5, 91; and interest group politics, 90; and liberal values, 50–1, 66–7, 72–3, 74, 78, 85; and political skills, 79–81; and political stability, 39, 43, 72, 117–18, 119
consensus, absence of, 34, 117–18
Cuba: ideological unified elite, 36; revolution, 31; and Third World, 104
Czechoslovakia, 43

Davis, R., 97n
de Jouvenel, B., 56n
democracy: and consensual unified elites, 37, 57, 117–18; development in Western societies, 57; and egalitarianism, 67; and elites, 58, 77–8, 117–18; failure to spread, 117–18; and liberalism, 56–68
Denmark: consensual unified elite, 40–1, 120; imperfectly unified elite, 50, 73, 121; socioeconomic development, 30; suppression of liberal practices in, 49
developed (Level 4) societies: class in, 32; dependence on developing societies, 100; and elite types, 77–8; illegal immigration to, 101; non-elite orientations in, 30, 43–6; problems

131

of, 31, 43–6, 96, 107–8; work-force
composition, 23, 125; in world
system, 98–9
developing (Level 2,3) societies: and
elite types, 38–41; food sources,
99–100; problems of, 101, 107–8;
work-force composition, 22–3; in
world system, 99
development, socioeconomic: and
capitalism, 96–8; in contemporary
societies, 24–5, 118–19, 122–4; end
of period of increasing resources,
106–8; history of, 96–9; levels of,
21–5; and non-elite orientations,
25–32; and world system, 96–9
Devlin, P., 54n
disunified elites: in Chile, 36; concept
of, 35–6, 38–9; consensual
unification of, 74–8, 91–3, 119–22;
and democracy, 73, 76–7; and
developed societies, 41–3; and
fascism, 36; and interest group
politics, 90; and liberal values, 73;
and political instability, 36; and
revolution, 36; in South Africa and
Zimbabwe Rhodesia, 79–80; *see
also* France; non-elites
Dorso, G., 4

Eastern Europe: communism in, 104;
ideological unified elite, 36, 74; as
semi-periphery, 99
elites: basis of, 32–5; and bureaucracy,
71–2; definition, 20; and developed
societies, 42–5, 108; and discrimination, 78–85; and freedom and
equality, 69–72; and ideology, 16–
17, 130; inevitability of, 70–2; and
insiders, 43–6, 95–6; and levels of
development, 21–2, 28–9, 31, 45,
108; and liberalism, 65–9; and non-
elites, 19–21, 25–6, 28–9, 35, 41,
44–6, 47, 77–8, 117–18; and
outsiders, 45; and politics, 77–8,
93–4, 117–18; and political stability,
46–7, 117–18; power of, 34–5; and
representative government, 50–1,
57–9, 77–8; and welfare statism,
15–17, 130; *see also* consensual
unified elites; disunified elites;
ideological unified elites;
imperfectly unified elites
elitism: acceptance today, 3–4;
classical exponents, 1–3, 18–19;
democratic theory of, 3; eclipse of,

4, 6–7; and elite consensual
unification, 119–22; and fascism, 1;
as intellectual orientation, 2–4; and
liberal values, 69; and normative
preferences, 69–74; and problems of
developed societies, 126; and Third
World development, 122; utility of
paradigm, 46–7, 69, 117–19; *see also*
democracy; Marxism
energy sources, 107–8
England: consensual unified elite, 38,
77–8, 120; liberalism in, 64;
revolution, 28; socioeconomic
development, 96; *see also* Great
Britain
equality: and elitism, 69, 72, 93; and
liberalism, 51, 56–67; limitations on,
70–2, 93; and socialism, 63–4, 67; as
value, 3–4, 109–10
Europe: historical development,
28–30; immigration to, 101; *per
capita* income, 99; political
instability in, 36; postwar
development, 11

fascism, 9–10, 29, 31–2, 36–7
Field, G. L., 20n, 24n, 25, 41n, 43n,
126n
France: anti-fascist coalition in, 9;
disunified elite, 35–6, 50;
imperfectly unified elite, 40–1, 73,
77–8; and imperialism, 111;
revolution, 28, 35–6; socioeconomic
development, 29–30, 38;
suppression of liberal practices in,
49; Third Republic, 76
freedom: cost of, 59; as objective
value, 3–4; and original liberalism,
56; society of free men, 59

Germany: disunified elite, 50; fascist
regime in, 29; ideological unified
elite, 74; socioeconomic
development, 29, 97–8; suppression
of liberal practices in, 49
Germino, D., 4
Gladstone, W., 54n
Great Britain: consensual unified elite,
50, 72, 118; discrimination in, 82;
and imperialism, 111–13; political
stability, 46–7; socioeconomic
development, 28–30; subnational
divisions in, 87–9
Grøholt, K., 20n, 43n

134 *Index*

Higley, J., 20n, 41n, 43n
Hobbes, T., 128–9
Holland, 50; *see also* Netherlands
House, E., 54, 68

ideological unified elites: concept of,
36–9; and developed societies, 43;
and interest group politics, 90; and
liberal values, 74; possibility of in
South Africa and Zimbabwe
Rhodesia, 79; possible
transformation of, 75
ideology, 'end of', 13
imperialism, 108–14
India, 112
Indo-China, 111–12, 113
Indonesia, 111–12
imperfectly unified elites: concept of,
39–41; creation of, 77; and
democracy, 58; and developed
societies, 41–3, 73, 77; and interest
group politics, 90; and liberal
values, 73; transformation of, 78
insiders: conflict with elites, 45–6,
95–6; conflict with outsiders, 31
Ireland, 88–9; *see also* Northern
Ireland
Italy: fascist regime in, 29, 74;
imperfectly unified elite, 41, 73, 77;
socioeconomic development, 29, 97;
suppression of liberal practices in,
49

Japan: imperfectly unified elite, 40–1,
73, 77; postwar recovery, 11;
socioeconomic development, 21, 29,
98

Kant, I., 128, 130
Kenya, 85
Keynes, J. M., 10
Kuwait, 25

Latin America: democracy in, 58, 118;
elite structure in, 50, 121;
imperialism in, 109; *per capita*
income, 99; as periphery, 99;
political instability in, 36, 121;
socioeconomic development, 28
liberal values, 56–65; and elite types,
50, 73–4; profession and practice of,
48–51; and representative politics,
48–51; and secessionist movements,
85–9

liberalism: and democracy, 56–68;
doctrinal degeneration of, 51–6; as
ideology, 13, 130; and elitism, 51,
65–6; and equality, 56–67; and
freedom, 56, 58–65; as paradigm,
7–13; and socialism, 8–13
Low Countries, 96

Machiavelli, N., 128–9
Malaya, 111
Malawi, 85
Marxism: and elitism, 18–19; and
revolutions, 28; and Russian
communism, 103
Meisel, J., 2n
Mexico, 38, 77
Michels, R., 1–4, 18–19
Middle East: and democracy, 58; and
elite structure, 50; *per capita*
income, 99; political instability in,
36; as semi-periphery, 99
Mosca, G., 1–4, 18–19

Netherlands: consensual unified elite,
38, 50, 118; discrimination in, 82;
and imperialism, 111–12;
socioeconomic development, 29–30;
suppression of liberal practices in,
49
New England colonies, 32
New Zealand: consensual unified elite,
38, 50; *per capita* income, 99;
socioeconomic development, 29–30
non-elites: in developed societies,
30–1, 43–6; and disunified elites,
35–6, 76–7, 118; lack of consensus
among, 117–18; orientations of, 19,
25–32, 47; and problems of Third
World, 108, 122–3; and secessionist
movements, 89; and socioeconomic
development, 118–19, 122–3; *see
also* elites
North Korea, 36, 104
North–South conflict, 96–102, 105–6
North Vietnam, 104; *see also* Indo-
China
Northern Ireland, 87–9
Norway: consensual unified elite,
40–1, 120–1; imperfectly unified
elite, 50, 73, 120; socialist
government, 8; socioeconomic
development, 14, 30; suppression of
liberal practices in, 49